The Art of Understanding and Communicating Effectively with Diverse People

BE DIVERSITY
COMPETENT!

Religion/Spirituality

Race/Ethnicity

Disabilities

Language

Culture

Gender

Age

Class

Education

Work Styles

Personalities

Body Orientation

Socio-Economics

Sexual Orientation

Jermaine M. Davis

D1384497

▪☐▪☐ About the Author
Jermaine M. Davis

Jermaine M. Davis grew up in a single-parent home in Chicago's housing projects. After losing six family members to street violence, he began studying success principles to change the direction of his life. Now, Jermaine is the author of six books including: Get Up Off Your Butt & Do It NOW, Leading with Greatness, 207 STAND OUT Quotes to Help You Succeed in Life, School & Work, You Don't Have to SELL OUT to STAND OUT, Be Diversity Competent and Lessons from the Road.

Jermaine earned a BA and an MA in Speech Communication and completed a second MA in Education. He is a Professor of Communication Studies at Century College in Minnesota and has been presented with the prestigious College Instructor of the Year Award. Jermaine is also CEO, Founder and President of two companies: Seminars & Workshops, Inc. and Snack Attack Vending of Minnesota.

Before becoming a professor and CEO of two companies, Jermaine learned effective communication and leadership skills from organizations including IBM, Rolm Telecommunications, Frito Lay, Inc. and the Keebler Company. Although he left his corporate positions for a professorship, he continues to be active in the corporate world through his professional keynotes and workshops. Jermaine is one of the country's most requested inspirational teachers in the areas of diversity competence, leadership, team building and sustaining personal and professional motivation.

Jermaine is a Chicago native and presently resides in St. Paul, MN.

ISBN 0-9673500-2-6

Library of Congress Cataloging-in-Publication Data has been filed for.

Manufactured and Printed in the United States of America

First Printing: August 2007

10 9 8 7 6 5 4 3 2 1

Jermaine M. Davis' books may be purchased in bulk for educational, business, fund-raising or sales promotional use. For information, please call (651) 487-7576 or e-mail jermaine@jermainedavis.com.

Jermaine M. Davis, Seminars & Workshops, Inc.
1259 Rose Vista Court
Roseville, MN 55113
(651) 487-7576
Visit: www.jermainedavis.com

Cover Design and Layout by Christina Frieler

▪☐▪☐ Table of Contents

▣ Part 4

" A fresh perspective teaching individuals
and organizations how to communicate
appropriately across differences! This
book will help leaders create an inclusive
and welcoming environment for all
employees. Jermaine Davis has built a
bridge across interpersonal and cross-
cultural challenges by helping us apply
the practical skills offered in this book. "

Herschel Herndon, Best Buy Co., Inc.
Vice President, Human Resources
Multicultural Relations and Diversity

■   ■   ■

Communication is the Beginning of Understanding.

As you read *Be Diversity Competent*, you will discover better ways of communicating and relating to diverse people. I encourage you to add new communication skills to your Diversity Toolbox to help you communicate and interact more effectively with individuals who are different from you. Remember, the best and most effective communicators are those who have multiple tools in their Diversity Toolbox. You can keep track of your newly acquired communication and diversity skills on pages 240 and 24l. Good success as you improve and increase your Diversity Competence in Life, School & Work.

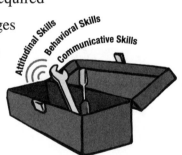

∎□∎□ Jermaine's Acknowledgements and Thank Yous

Be *Diversity Competent* is fully dedicated to ALL the women and men who died in the struggle fighting for human rights, civil rights, social justice and freedom for ALL people. This book is also dedicated to those who fought for human equality in the past, the present and for those who will fight for justice in the future. I want to pay special homage to the individuals who relentlessly, day after day, week after week and year after year deliberately advocate for the rights of ALL women and men. I would personally like to thank each and every diversity trainer, speaker, consultant and facilitator around the globe who are toiling to make our schools, organizations, houses of faith and worship, neighborhoods and society a better place to live, work and play. Thank you for all of your dedication, determination and discipline to keep on keeping on even when you feel like giving up and throwing in the towel.

While conducting research for and writing *Be Diversity Competent*, I have developed a deeper affinity and a special appreciation for the white women and men who historically advocated for the rights of African slaves. Wow–it took great diversity courage from the white slave abolitionists who argued and fought for the rights and freedom of African slaves. Despite the profitable institution of slavery, a few white women and men committed to justice and equality created the Underground Railroad during one of the most disturbing times in American history. The Underground Railroad was an awesome system that allowed enslaved human beings a chance at human freedom. Without the Underground Railroad I may never have heard of people like Harriet Tubman and Frederick Douglas as well as many other unsung heroes who gained freedom through the Underground Railroad. These white women and men were courageous enough to risk their own lives and the lives of their families (many were killed) to ensure freedom for all people. The descendants of the white slave abolitionists should be proud to be descendants of people with such heroic spirit. Thank you again!

Thanks to my mother, Carolyn "Charmaine" Davis, who modeled diversity competence to the best of her abilities. I thank you, Mom, because you deliberately taught me my very first diversity competent skill, which was the Golden Rule. Mom, thanks for being a great diversity role model for fifty-three years. I never heard you tell or make one racist, sexist or homophobic joke or comment. I remember when I first introduced you to all my diverse friends that I had met while in college, you created a diversity-friendly, inclusive and welcoming environment for them in our small two bedroom apartment on the west side of Chicago. You were truly practicing the philosophy of diversity competence well before *Be Diversity Competent* was ever conceived. Thanks for the great diversity guidance and leadership.

Katie Ruberto (a.k.a., M.B.A. Katie), the phrase thank you is not strong enough to communicate my appreciation and gratitude for your commitment and dedication to *Be Diversity Competent*. You pushed me, encouraged me and believed in me when I felt like giving up at times. I am blessed to have you on my Dream Team. You did great work! You bring the best out of me when we work together. Thanks for sharing your editorial perspectives and insights. You are all over this book, and I am glad that you were able to help me manifest my vision for *Be Diversity Competent*. Thank you for being a great friend, both personally and professionally. Good successes in all you do!

Chris Traxler, you were determined to help me with *Be Diversity Competent*. Thanks for ALWAYS adjusting your schedule to accommodate my busy speaking and teaching schedule. You always help me understand my perspectives and philosophies better after we meet at Barnes & Noble. Thank you for your editing help, and I hope to work with you again, and again and again.

Loli Dillon – Thanks! I appreciate your willingness to listen to my concerns and understand my vision for the book before jumping into the project. I appreciate your fast turn around time especially when I had tight deadlines. Thank you for your editorial insights and advice.

Christina Frieler, I am fortunate to work with such a talented woman once again. Thank you for your creative design work. Thank you for listening to my request and understanding my vision for *Be Diversity Competent*. I love how you take my ideas and help me illustrate them in such an artistic manner. Thank you for sharing your TAGS (Talents, Abilities, Gifts and Skills) with me once again.

Cheri Edwards, thank you for helping me articulate and capture the essence of each story written in *Be Diversity Competent!*

Thanks to all my friends, family members and colleagues who continuously support and believe in me as well as my dreams, goals and aspirations. I appreciate each and every one of you who continue to love and befriend me even in the midst of my highs and lows, successes and failures. I love each and every one of you. Thanks!

■   ■   ■

◼◻◼◻ The Genesis of
Be Diversity Competent!

D iversity, diversity, diversity. Diversity is a reality. No, let me try that again: Diversity is a truth, a fact and a hardcore reality.

I was sitting in Caribou Coffee on May 18, 2006, at 4:13 p.m., attempting to write the opening thoughts to *Be Diversity Competent*, and I was struggling with how to best construct the emotional and intellectual tone for the book. I kept asking myself two questions: Should I take a radical and revolutionary approach to convey my ideas and philosophies around the topic of diversity? Or, should I lessen the blow to make the book more palatable for readers to process, grasp and eventually put into action?

> "Learning is not attained by chance. It must be sought for with ardor and attended to with diligence."
> **Abigail Adams**

As I played intellectual ping-pong, going back and forth and trying to answer these questions, for how to construct the book, a biblical scripture immediately popped inside of my head. It states, "Be wise as a serpent and harmless as a dove." As I decoded the scripture, the residual message remaining was to proceed *strategically* when writing and constructing this book. The diversity ideas shared in this book are among some of my most personal writings. I have made myself personally and professionally vulnerable because I want desperately to help individuals and organizations move from diversity awareness to diversity action and implementation.

I was then equipped with the idea but I was still unsure of how to proceed strategically. Then, I had an *Ah-Ha* moment (An *Ah-Ha* moment is flashes of insight that will change your life forever, as defined by Oprah Winfrey). I could hear the voice of my mother, saying to me when I was younger, "Tell it like it is, Baby. You've got to call it like you see it. Call an ace an ace and a spade a spade. Tell it like it is." One of my *Ah-Ha* moments, which arose from the biblical scripture and from my mother's perspective on truth telling, was to write *Be Diversity Competent* from a reality-based approach and perspective, but most importantly, to write it *strategically* using parts of my own academic training, corporate and social service experience and interpersonal wisdom.

Be Diversity Competent is about helping individuals and organizations communicate appropriately, competently and effectively across differences by willingly learning to understand the differences of diverse people. This book is written for those who desire to create respectful and inclusive environments within their communities, houses of faith and worship, organizations, schools and society in general. I wrote this book to assist those who *already* explore and embrace diversity and for those who are unclear on how to *begin* the process of exploring and embracing diversity. Lastly, it was written for those who agree and accept that diversity exists and that its ongoing presence impacts the way we all live, play and work.

Individuals and organizations cannot become diversity competent if they do not acknowledge and admit that diversity is a universal truth and a hardcore reality. I truly believe what I wrote in my second book, *Leading with Greatness,* "You cannot grow in life, school and work when you avoid, deny, minimize and resist reality." Diversity competence begins with the willingness to deal with the reality of diversity. I look forward to seeing and hearing of your progress as you grow and develop on your diversity journey and/or diversity quest.

> "Take the attitude of a student, never be too big to ask questions,
> never know too much to learn something new."
> **Og Mandino**

■   ■   ■

Part 1

The Art of Understanding and Communicating Effectively with Diverse People

Uncle Ricky and Me: A Missed Opportunity

As a child, I grew up in a fatherless home with my mother and siblings, Greg and Katrina. My mother desperately wanted me to have positive male guidance and leadership in my life so she regularly sent me to visit with one of my five uncles every other weekend during the school year and every weekend during the summer months. My favorite uncle at the time was my Uncle Ricky. Uncle Ricky was a bon-a-fide salesman who purchased wholesale merchandise in an area of Chicago known as "Jew Town" and resold it on the streets of Chicago at retail prices.

He was the first person who taught me how to make money through entrepreneurial efforts within the system of capitalism. I credit him for all of my entrepreneurial efforts and endeavors today. In fact, with me along for company, Uncle Ricky would sell his merchandise or 'merch' as he called it, throughout the entire city of Chicago, but he preferred to hustle his 'merch' mostly on the south side of Chicago. We traveled throughout the big city, ate fast food, played video games and conversed. Oftentimes, Uncle Ricky shared with me his stories, ideologies and philosophies regarding life. It was during these times that Uncle Ricky began planting negative seeds of racial fear, hate and uncertainty inside my seven-year old innocent and easily impressionable mind.

Uncle Ricky would declare, "Jermaine, the white man is *scaaandalous*, man! Don't trust the white man! They're out to get you!" Then he would add with his voice at a lower octave, *"The white man is the Devil manifested in the flesh."*

That statement was the final straw; I had to find out what he meant with his emotional statements. At the age of seven, I had no idea what *'the Devil manifested in the flesh'* meant, but it didn't sound good. So with great curiosity, I asked my grandmother what it all meant, as I told her the comments Uncle Ricky shared with me about 'the white man.'

"Why didn't you tell me this earlier?" my grandmother asked before she began her explanation. She told me that Uncle Ricky had gone away to college in Oklahoma on an academic scholarship, and because he was naturally talented in engineering, mathematics and science, he was expected to do well. My grandmother explained, "While walking back to his campus apartment after class one evening, your Uncle Ricky was jumped, kicked and beaten badly by four white guys while they screamed and yelled racial epithets at him. After that racial incident, he abandoned his scholarship, aborted his career goals and aspirations and failed to complete his education. He came back to Chicago with nothing but anger and vindictiveness toward white people and white men, specifically."

My Uncle Ricky had a terrible diversity experience with a group of white men and never dealt with the resulting diversity conflict and tension in a constructive and healthy manner. He left his feelings toward white people unattended, which intensified and began to escalate into strong feelings of racial dislike, disgust and distrust. These negative feelings simmered and set in, finally turning into racial resentment and bitterness; Uncle Ricky had become hardened toward white people.

My uncle wanted nothing to do with white people, often telling me, "Jermaine, I will never, ever work for the white man, and I will *deal* with them *only* if I have to." He did, in fact, interact with white men, but it was forced because he had to buy his wholesale merchandise from them. My uncle's mismanaged anger became a barrier to his ability to communicate and interact effectively with white people. He died with racial anger still festering inside his heart and mind; the fact that he never overcame his racial anger prevented him from communicating and interacting with white people competently and effectively.

Unfortunately, Uncle Ricky died *diversity incompetent (diversity incompetence is the unwillingness or inability to communicate competently across differences)*. I often think about the time we spent together on the weekends, and how he missed out on many opportunities to steer me in the right direction regarding diversity issues and effective diversity communication. I miss Uncle Ricky immensely, and if I had the opportunity to teach him what I know *now* about being diversity competent as an individual, I would do it in a heartbeat. Instead, Uncle Ricky died a prisoner of his personal Diversity BAPS (Biases, Assumptions, Prejudices and Stereotypes). It was Uncle Ricky's Diversity BAPS that prevented him from becoming diversity competent.

How many Uncle Rickys do you know on a personal and professional level? How many Uncle Rickys do you interact with on a daily basis who are employed as accountants, bankers, church officials, computer professionals, counselors, customer service representatives, doctors, human resource professionals, investigators, journalists, judges, lawyers, loan officers, news reporters, paramedics, police officers, policy makers, politicians, probation officers, real estate agents, sales associates, school administrators, social workers, sports professionals, teachers, therapists and so on? The responses that I get in my workshops based on these questions are alarming. Even the workshop participants are surprised at the amount of people in their life that fit the description of being diversity incompetent.

Can You Please Explain
This Diversity Stuff to Me?

Diversity encompasses all the characteristics and qualities that make individuals uniquely different and similar. In American history, whether people accepted it or not, the formal and informal study of diversity became necessary as communities, houses of faith and worship, organizations, schools and society as a whole became increasingly diverse. This increase in diversity was represented culturally, ethnically, linguistically and racially. Other dimensions of diversity that were often overlooked or made voiceless and invisible, such as gays and lesbians, persons with disabilities and diverse religious and spiritual communities also became more deliberate about having their diversity known, validated and recognized. The people who represent the overlooked dimensions of diversity want and deserve a voice, acknowledgement and visibility within their communities, houses of faith and worship, organizations, schools and society.

Why regard and study diversity as a society? Simply put, diversity affects, impacts, influences and permeates all the various facets of our lives. Diversity will touch the willing and unwilling, the proponents and opponents, the cheerleaders and the cynics. I once heard diversity expert and president of The American Institute for Managing Diversity and author of *Beyond Race and Gender*, Dr. R. Roosevelt Thomas, Jr., make a profound statement during a diversity presentation. He stated, "The more diverse an organization becomes, the more that organization will have to look at and consider doing things differently if that organization *really* wants to succeed." He was implying that organizations must consider doing things fundamentally different, as they become more and more diverse. Embracing diversity is a real business necessity and not an option or a nice *thing* to do. Dr. Thomas' goal was to communicate to organizations that the very idea of a diverse organization implies there will be some level of diversity conflict and tension at some point in time. However, having more organizational diversity does not mean the organization is doomed and headed for destruction. It does mean the organization must become diversity competent to deal appropriately and effectively with their new dimensions of diversity.

Making fundamental diversity changes within an organization means that people within the organization will have to analyze the diversity history and structure of their organization. Conducting and performing a diversity analysis requires that the organization look meticulously at how they define diversity as well as their diversity philosophy, policies, practices and procedures they currently have in place. In order for this type of analysis to take place, the organization has to do more than pay lip service to diversity efforts and initiatives; there has to be a visible commitment made by leaders within the organization.

As you begin your diversity analysis, there are a series of questions that you should consider to help you through your research. These questions will assist you as you explore how to make your organization or school more diversity-friendly, inclusive and welcoming.

Questions for Conducting a Diversity Analysis

Explore the visible structure of your organization or school:

- Do you have a diverse group of employees or student population? Why or why not?

- Do you have a diverse management or administrative team? Why or why not?

- Do you have a diverse board of directors? Why or why not?

- Do you have diverse representation at all levels within your organization? Why or why not?

Explore the recruiting and retention efforts of your organization or school:

- How aggressive are your marketing efforts for attracting and recruiting diverse talent?

- What systems do you have in place to retain diverse individuals once you've attracted, recruited, hired and/or enrolled them within your organization?

- How do you handle diversity-related issues within your organization or school?

- How do you personally and professionally address colleagues, leaders and students who violate diversity-related policies and procedures?

- Is your organization or school culture welcoming of diverse individuals? If so, how? If not, why?

- Can diverse candidates maintain their unique diversity and individuality without being personally and professionally penalized? Explain.

- Does your organization or school have supplier diversity programs in place?

Explore your role in creating a diversity-friendly, inclusive and welcoming environment within your organization or school:

- Can you clearly explain the benefits of a diverse organization or school?

- What are you doing as an organization to ensure that diverse people are included in roles and positions that they have not typically held in the past?

Organizations, schools and individuals who answer these questions positively are not completely absent of diversity conflict and tension, but they demonstrate a commitment to creating diversity-friendly, inclusive and welcoming environments for all their colleagues, employees and students to thrive and succeed. The organizations that are proactive about addressing and dealing with diversity issues tend to experience less diversity conflict and tension. ***Diversity conflict and tension arises when diverse individuals' needs, wants and expectations are unmet or violated.*** Diversity leaders must become competent regarding how to deal with diversity conflict and tension to extinguish diversity fires appropriately and effectively. By anticipating potential diversity issues and conflicts and revisiting your diversity expectations on a regular basis, you and your organization will be able to effectively intervene and significantly minimize diversity conflict and tension.

When I think of individuals and organizations that are diversity proactive, I think of visionaries because they anticipate what could lead to diversity conflict and tension before it happens. Proactive individuals and organizations are regularly planning ahead and thinking of strategies on how to create diversity-friendly, inclusive and welcoming environments. They prepare to embrace the new diversity entering into their school or workplace.

On the other hand, reactive organizations are always scrambling to figure out what to do when diversity conflict and tension manifests among colleagues and employees or when someone shows anger and frustration around a diversity-related issue after it has already occurred. Being proactive about diversity-related issues and topics is no different or less important than preparing for hazardous emergencies or unexpected quality control issues. Ideally, diversity preparedness should be a part of an organization's ongoing goals and processes.

Reactive individuals and organizations refuse to accept that their neighborhoods and organizations are rapidly changing. *Reactive* individuals and organizations deal with diversity conflict and tension in three destructive ways: (1) through diversity avoidance, (2) diversity denial and (3) diversity minimization. In other words, they ignore the reality of diversity because they are unwilling to learn new approaches to behaving and communicating effectively with the "newness" within their organization. Many are aware of diversity facts and figures due to demographical and statistical data, but they still refuse to plan ahead or budget accordingly. Those who avoid, deny and minimize diversity are the individuals and organizations that are most often forced to deal with diversity in a court of law. This can be due to class action lawsuits driven by inappropriate comments, unprofessional behaviors and unfair and unethical hiring practices.

Now, ask yourself the following questions: Which kind of diversity practitioner am I when it comes to embracing the reality of diversity? Am I proactive or reactive? What is the cost of being diversity proactive or diversity reactive to an individual or an organization?

Has Society Really Changed?

Perhaps a few individuals and organizations need to be reminded that we are surrounded by diversity on an ongoing basis. Consider how the various dimensions of diversity have changed the composition of the United States of America in the following statistical examples:

- There are 39.7 million blacks in the U.S., and there is a projected increase to 61.4 million by July 2050 (U.S. Census Bureau, 2006).

- There are 14 million Asian Americans in the U.S., and there is a projected increase to 33.4 million by July 2050 (U.S. Census Bureau, 2006).

- There are 42.7 million Hispanics in the U.S., and the Hispanic population is projected to triple in size by 2050 (U.S. Census Bureau, 2006 and Hispanic Trends, 2005).

- There were about 4.6 million people in the U.S. who are American Indian and Alaska Native or American Indian and Alaska Native in combination with one or more other races, making up 1.5% of the total population (U.S. Census Bureau, 2006).

- The Native American population will grow by 51.4%, outpacing the projected gains of 32.4% for the black population, 24.2% for the total U.S. population and 17.6% for the white population. Also, the Native American population is relatively young. Census 2000 indicates that the median age of Native Americans is 28 years (Selig Center, 2005).

- According to a survey conducted by the *Washington Post*, the Henry J. Kaiser Family Foundation and Harvard University, 53 percent of whites, 77 percent of blacks, 68 percent of Latinos and 67 percent of Asians said that they had no racial preference for a spouse. Out of 1,709 nationwide participants in the study, 4 out of 10 people reported having dated someone outside their race.

- Women-owned businesses are growing at twice the rate of all privately held firms (Center for Women's Business Research).

- Women of Color and Work: Labor force participation rates for women, by race, were: black, 61.6%; white, 58.9%; Asian, 58.2%; and Hispanic, 55.3% (WOW! Facts, 2006).

- Women obtain 50% of all undergraduate business degrees (International Association for Management Education).

- Women are more likely to register to vote in every state but Pennsylvania (WOW! Facts, 2006).

- There are 37 million women of color in the United States workforce. Women of color represent 15% of America's private-sector workforce (Spellman College, 2004 and The U.S. Equal Employment Opportunity Commission, 2002).

- African-Americans earned $670 billion in 2004 and their buying power is expected to reach $1 trillion in 2010 (WOW! Facts 2006 and Essence, 2005).

- There were 1.2 million African-American owned businesses in 2002, up 45% from 1997 (U.S. Census Bureau, 2005).

- Among blacks age 25 and over, 17% had a bachelor's degree or higher in 2003 (WOW! Facts, 2006).

- 20% of Asian Americans ages 25 and older have an advanced degree (e.g., master's, PhD, MD or JD) (U.S. Census Bureau, 2006).

- There were 1.1 million Asian-owned businesses in 2002, up 24% from 1997 (U.S. Census Bureau, 2006).

- Asian Americans own more than 35% of the nation's hotel properties (Entrepreneur.com, 2004).

- Asian workers of both sexes earned more than their white, black, Hispanic and Latino counterparts in 2003 and their median household income is the highest among all race groups (U.S. Bureau of Labor Statistics, 2004).

- Asian American buying power was $397 billion in 2005 and is expected to reach $579 billion in 2010 (Selig Center, 2005).

- By 2025, the number of Spanish-speaking Hispanics in the U.S. will reach 40.2 million, up from 27.8 million today (New Age Media Concepts, 2005).

- Native American buying power was $51.1 billion in 2005 and is expected to reach $69.2 billion in 2010 (Selig Center, 2005).

- 11 out of 50 states in the U.S. have at least half a million Hispanics (U.S. Census Bureau, 2005).

- More than seven hundred thousand (714,000) Hispanics 25 years and older had advanced degrees in 2004 (e.g., master's professional, doctorate) (U.S. Census Bureau, 2005).

- The buying power of Hispanics was $736 billion in 2005 and is expected to reach $1.87 trillion in 2010 (Selig Center, 2005).

- There were 1.6 million Hispanic-owned businesses in 2002, up 31% from 1997 (U.S. Census Bureau, 2005).

- About 51.2 million people in the U.S. have some level of disability. They represent 18% of the population (U.S. Census Bureau, 2006).

- Forty-two percent (42%) of working-age men (21 to 64) who have disabilities are employed, while 34% of working age women who are disabled are employed. These percentages translate to 4.0 million disabled working men and 3.5 million disabled women who are employed (Newswire, 2005).

- About 36% of adults with disabilities reported going out to shows, movies, sports events or club meetings. There are 24 million registered voters who are disabled (National Organization on Disability, 2004).

- The 2000 Census reported 1.2 million people in the U.S. in same-sex relationships.

- *Diversity Best Practices* predicts the purchasing power of the GLBT population will reach $750 billion in 2008 and $1 trillion in 2012 (Diversity Best Practices, 2006).

- Most of the demographic analyses that have been carried out affirm that there are high levels of educational attainment among gay men and lesbians; in addition, the typical gay-male and lesbian couple neighborhood has a higher proportion of college graduates (among adults 25 and older) than the typical heterosexual unmarried partner and married couple neighborhood (The Urban Institute, 2004).

- There were 35.2 million foreign-born persons (legal and illegal in the U.S. in March 2005). This is the highest number ever recorded (Center for Immigration Studies, 2005).

- Immigrants account for 12.1 % of the total population, the highest percentage in eight decades (Center for Immigration Studies, 2005).

- In 2005, foreign-born workers made up about 15% of the U.S. civilian labor force age 16 and over (U.S. Bureau of Labor Statistics, 2006).

- About 11% of immigrants are self-employed, compared with 13% of natives (Center for Immigration Studies, 2005).

The demographic changes in the United States are having wide-reaching implications in most communities. For example, in a diverse school or district, the cafeteria will need to address and revisit their meal plans to avoid excluding a particular cultural or ethnic group. A few other examples include:

- Grocery stores are at an economic advantage if they are proactive and capitalize on changes within their community demographics. They will secure their economic success by taking the time to understand the community demographics and adapting their product offerings to meet the needs of their customers.

- Retailers that have a national presence should regularly assess their customer demographics to ensure that their local advertising and product assortment mirror the needs of the community. An example would be in music selection. It is important for a store to avoid offering a selection of music by only Mexican artists in a predominantly Puerto Rican or Argentinean community.

Respecting and catering to the cultural and ethnic needs and desires demonstrated in the previous examples explains how a business can explore and embrace new and different dimensions of diversity. A business savvy and diversity competent employee or leader understands that different cultural and ethnic groups often have different needs. It is only practical and economically sensible to address those needs through changes in the environment and based on the needs of their customers.

On a social level, diversity affects many aspects of one's personal and professional life. Consider the case of a teacher who must determine the best way to teach and reach a diverse group of students. She or he must regard diversity when making selections of teaching materials and curricula. The content a teacher uses within a diverse classroom is extremely important because classroom curricula can make diverse students feel welcome or unwelcome and included or excluded. It is imperative for every individual, no matter what her or his profession is, to ask and answer the question, "How will diversity affect, impact and influence the way I do my job?" I had to ask and answer this question myself, as a college professor, business owner, author and professional speaker.

Although many individuals and organizations agree that demographic changes have occurred and that diversity really exists, there are still many individuals that fail to see how diversity affects their personal, professional and private lives. I have found that many individuals have a one-dimensional view and a singular definition of diversity. Some individuals define and limit the scope of diversity to issues of race and gender exclusively. Yes, I do agree that the United States of America has a long history of racism and sexism; however, being diversity competent vigorously implies that there are other dimensions of diversity that need to be recognized, acknowledged and regarded if individuals and organizations truly want to create diversity-friendly, inclusive and welcoming environments. We will continue to explore these other dimensions of diversity in detail throughout the remainder of the book.

Why Can't We All Just Get Along?

After the first break of a three-hour *Be Diversity Competent* workshop for a group of city, county and state administrators, I stated jokingly, but still maintaining a sense of seriousness, "Are there any questions, concerns, rebukes or rebuttals before we transition to our next topic?" There was one city official who raised his hand and replied, "My question is, I am responsible for overseeing 139 diverse city employees, and I have 21 direct reports, and I *really* want to know why can't we all just get along for God's sake? We're all people...we're all just plain ole' human beings." As I maintained respectful eye contact during the city official's emotional question, his facial expression was one of despair. I replied, "We can't get along with individuals that we do not understand. We can't get along with people that we only *tolerate* during diversity encounters. We can't get along with people with whom we are afraid of communicating and interacting with. We can't get along with individuals when they perceive their diversity is *not* wanted, recognized and/or respected. We can't get along with diverse groups of people when they feel demeaned, devalued, dishonored and disrespected, both personally and professionally. We can't get along with people if we are not willing to really—and I mean *really*—get along with them. To get along with someone requires time, effort and dedication." After my response to his question, the city official nodded his head in agreement still maintaining a facial expression of despair and concern.

I shared with the administrators that when all colleagues and employees, no matter what dimension of diversity they represent, feel and perceive their diversity is being demeaned, devalued, dishonored and disrespected, conflict within the organization will be inevitable. Throughout *Be Diversity Competent*, I refer to this as diversity conflict and tension. As organizations become increasingly diverse, managing diversity conflict and tension competently is a crucial aspect of every leader's position.

The way diversity conflict and tension is dealt with within an organization will determine if that organization becomes a diversity-friendly, inclusive and welcoming organization. Unfortunately, most people are generally conflict avoidant, and when you add diversity conflict and tension to the equation, they become increasingly fearful; this leads to diversity incompetent organizations. After considering this, I have a diversity conflict question for you to ponder: Is diversity conflict constructive or destructive, good or bad, positive or negative?

Defining Diversity

As highlighted before, *diversity is the characteristics and qualities that make individuals uniquely different and similar.* Each of us walks the planet with our own special and unique "diversity," and through our diversity, we present a sort of fingerprint of who we are. Although we may share similarities and basic characteristics, like the unique pattern of a fingerprint, no two of us are exactly alike. We are all fundamentally different from each other, and embracing this paradigm is critical to becoming diversity competent in life, school and work. This phenomenon reminds me of a profound observation communicated to me in 1996 by a fifth grader, who stated, "If all of us are the same, Mr. Jermaine, then a few of us are not needed." At the age of ten, this young man already understood the meaning of diversity and, in turn, recognized its value and ability to enrich the human experience.

Today, it is more important than ever to study diversity. Decades ago, predictions that the U.S. would become a "mosaic and kaleidoscope" of cultural diversity have become realized. All levels of schools and universities are accepting students with varying ethnic backgrounds, cultural practices, belief systems and sexual orientations. While these students still may find little change in the acceptance they receive, recognition of their existence *has* changed, particularly with the formation of student organizations to represent the various kinds of diverse groups.

This phenomenon is also producing an increasingly diverse workplace. As a result, corporations now need to assess recruitment procedures, hiring criteria and career advancement practices. There is also a need to evaluate regulations around workplace recognition of religious holidays. Many are finding that the days of traditional gift exchanges and Easter festivities no longer appeal to or are appropriate for the diverse workforce they now employ.

Many organizations are beginning to embrace the new diversity represented in the marketplace. These organizations have established and created employee resource groups and affinity groups as a network of support and a resource to help employees succeed within the dominant organizational culture. *Employee resource groups and affinity groups are defined as groups of employees or students that come together to form a network based on similar dimensions of diversity.* Employee resource groups and affinity groups support the recruitment and retention of diverse employees and students as well as innovation efforts of new products and services to support diverse demographics. The fact that employee resource groups and affinity groups exist within many organizations is an acknowledgement by organizational leaders that diversity is a societal fact and a hardcore reality.

In fact, all individuals find their daily life increasingly influenced by diversity. These days, people you call your "neighbors" may not resemble your ethnic group, speak your language or share your beliefs and values. These issues of diversity are no longer just limited to urban environments but are part of suburban and rural areas as well.

It is not our similarities that create diversity conflict and tension between diverse groups but our real and perceived differences. As human beings, we naturally migrate to those within our own comfort zone, most often seeking out those like ourselves. Intercultural scholars refer to those we feel most comfortable with as our "in-group." *In-groups are groups of individuals and communities of diversity we identify with and relate to.* The challenge becomes when we meet or work with someone outside of our comfort zone; we may fail to see that person as an individual. If we lack education and experience around different dimensions of diversity we are not familiar with; most individuals will communicate and interact with others based on group membership rather than on individual differences. In other words, we will communicate and interact with an individual based on the stereotypes we have learned of them within our community or what we see and hear from the media. With this type of influence, we have the potential to exclude an individual's true character and personality because we are blinded by a stereotype of their cultural background or ethnic group.

For example, when I was younger, I never had contact with anyone who was Asian, and the only information I possessed of Asians was from watching Bruce Lee and martial arts movies. When I finally encountered an Asian person, the first thought that registered in my mind was that all Asian people were great in martial arts; I admit I used to believe all Asians knew karate! People usually conclude that if a person is not like us, they must be radically different, and if we perceive individuals as too different from us, we are less likely to explore, welcome and embrace their diversity.

Aren't We More Similar Than Different?

Over a three-day period, I was invited to give five *Be Diversity Competent* presentations at a university in upstate New York. These presentations were designed for classified staff, professional staff and senior administrators of the university. During a break period in the second day of training, a guy named Ed caught up with me.

Ed acknowledged, "While I like what you're saying here, I have one disagreement with the content."

"Please share it," I said.

Ed looked me squarely in the eyes and asked, "Would you say as human beings we are more alike and similar than different?"

I thought about his question for a moment, before replying, "Depends on the meaning and context of your question."

Ed provided this example, "If I cut my hand as a white man, I bleed red blood, and if you cut yours, as a black man, you bleed red blood too."

With a smile, I said, "I'm no hematologist, but yes, with my limited knowledge of blood DNA, I would agree with that statement."

Then, Ed submitted, "So why are you spending most of your training time educating us on our differences rather than our similarities?"

I replied, "I agree, it's true most people do have much more in common than we think. However, Ed, people don't have conflict in life, school and work over their similarities. *People have conflict over their differences.* It is our differences and our inability to deal with those differences appropriately, competently and effectively that lead to diversity conflict and tension. And, if we ignore differences, it only leads to more diversity collisions because people bring their differences with them when they enter the workplace or step onto a college campus."

I continued, "Gary Chapman, author of *The Five Love Languages*, shares recent marriage statistics documenting that 50% of first marriages end in divorces, 60% of second marriages end in divorce, and 75% of third marriages end in divorce." I asked, "Do you know one of the main reason couples say their relationships end?"

Ed responded, "Irreconcilable differences?"

"Absolutely and exactly," I stated, zealously. "These marriages don't end because couples have issues with their similarities; they end because *they have issues over their differences, and they couldn't reconcile their differences.* The individuals in the relationship were either unwilling or unable to deal with their differences."

I continued, "Ed, those who can maneuver and work through their differences appropriately, competently and effectively will experience greater relationship satisfaction."

I explained, "Those who explore, acknowledge and respect differences can often sustain personal and workplace relationships indefinitely. The same principle is applicable when dealing with difficult diversity issues and resolving diversity conflict and tension. By exploring, acknowledging and respecting differences, you create better schools and organizations for students and employees to thrive and succeed in."

Ed replied by saying, "I see your point, Jermaine."

The more individuals and organizations stop exploring, acknowledging and respecting differences, the more you will see an increase of diversity conflict and tension in the workplace and school settings. Individuals and organizations filled with diversity conflict and tension make for less creative and innovative work environments and that can affect the bottom line. In fact, not dealing with diversity can snowball, eventually having a huge effect on the organization.

The Similarity Factor

Ed's perspective of focusing on our human similarities in order to build social and workplace harmony is not a distant thought. I agree with Ed's perspective and I teach in my communication courses that finding our human commonalities, likenesses and similarities are keys to cultivating strong and sustainable personal and professional relationships.

I often travel as a professional speaker and author, and I regularly find myself engaged in airport conversation with hundreds of strangers. So what is my approach to connecting with diverse women and men in the various airports around the world? I begin by asking questions to detect and discover our commonalities, likenesses and similarities. I refer to the questions that I ask of new and diverse individuals as "get to know you" questions. Consider the following questions after a nice, friendly and welcoming greeting.

Get to Know You Questions

• What type of work are you in that allows you to travel?

• Where is your home base or where do you reside?

• Do you travel for leisure as well?

- Where's your favorite place to travel or vacation?

- What do you do for fun?

- Do you have any hobbies? If so, what are they?

- Are you a native of the city or state where you presently reside?

- What are some of the attractions or culture of your city or state?

- What do you like most or least about your profession?

- Are you a sports fan? Which sport? Who's your favorite team or player?

I randomly employ these questions when seeking to establish common ground with new individuals that I encounter on my journey in life, school and work. The key to discovering similarities between you and others is to ask sincere questions that you genuinely desire to know the answers to and *listen* to the other person's answers and responses. This act of sincere question asking and listening will allow you to engage in further dialogue with the person you are interacting with.

Dealing with Diversity

Dealing with diversity on an interpersonal level begins by asking ourselves, "How are we similar?" It requires that we ask ourselves just how much alike we are as human beings if we are to set aside our differences. On a genetic level, and for scientific purposes, the human genome is the same for all humans. While we each have a unique genetic blueprint that makes us who we are, the differences are so slight they are insignificant to the mapping process.

Accordingly, if I needed a heart transplant, doctors would find a match for me based on the donor's size, blood type and tissue type. Traits like race, gender, religious preference or sexual orientation are simply unimportant in life-threatening situations. Nevertheless, these same traits become significant when we think about who our neighbors are, who we prefer working with or who gets the "big" promotion in the workplace.

So What Really Makes Us Different and Similar as Human Beings?

Examples of diversity characteristics and qualities making human beings different and similar are represented on this partial diversity list below. I have highlighted in bold the characteristics and qualities that I consider to be primary dimensions of diversity:

• **Abilities**	• Geography
• **Age**	• Language (accents and dialects)
• Beliefs	
• **Body Orientation (size and shape)**	• Nationality
	• Personalities
• Class (social or economic)	• **Race**
• Culture	• Religion/Spirituality
• Education	• **Sexual Orientation**
• **Ethnicity**	• Socio-Economics
• **Disabilities**	• Values
• **Gender**	• Work Styles

Because the primary dimensions of diversity most often involve physical characteristics or what I refer to as "identifiable characteristics," they are more difficult for some individuals to "see past or move beyond" when looking at someone different from ourselves.

The Primary Dimensions of Diversity

Primary dimensions of diversity are characteristics and qualities that consist of an individual's physical attributes (identifiable characteristics), early socializations (life teachings and indoctrinations) and life altering experiences (defining moments). These characteristics and qualities are considered primary because they either exist at birth or occur because of a significant life altering event or experience.

I initially learned of the primary dimensions of diversity when I read the groundbreaking diversity book, *Workforce America*, written by Marilyn Loden and Judy B. Rosener. They define primary dimensions of diversity as, ***"Those immutable human differences that are inborn and/or that exert an important impact on our early socialization and have an ongoing impact throughout our lives."*** Loden and Rosener write about how our primary dimensions of diversity are key in shaping our self-image and perceptions of how we view the world. They list the six primary dimensions of diversity as: age, ethnicity, gender, physical abilities/qualities, race and sexual/affectional orientation.

I have learned from conducting hundreds of diversity workshops and trainings that the primary dimensions of diversity are not without controversy. The most controversial is the subject matter of sexual orientation. For example, some individuals believe sexual orientation is not a primary trait existing at birth but instead is a lifestyle choice that can be easily reversed through repentance, religious prayer and spiritual counseling. Sexual orientation is an extremely divisive topic in our nation; it is an issue where both sides are strongly in favor of their own belief system. *Be Diversity Competent* was not written to debate an individual's sexual orientation; the goal of this book is to prevent discrimination from occurring in life, school and work and help individuals and organizations communicate more appropriately and effectively with diverse people.

Competent and effective communication becomes difficult when individuals get stuck on and cannot move past an individual's primary dimension of diversity. Consider the following examples:

• A first-year college student is excited about leaving home to attend college, live in the residence halls and meet her or his new roommate. Upon arrival at their dorm room, she or he discovers that their college roommate is visually impaired. How do you think this person will respond? Does having a visually impaired roommate prevent the other roommate from communicating and interacting competently and effectively? Can she or he get past their visually impaired roommates' primary dimension of diversity or will they get stuck on the roommate's disability?

- Evelyn, the president of a shipping company who is excited about the new vice president she's hired (Patty), discovers six weeks later that Patty is in a same-sex relationship. Evelyn is a devote Christian and believes same-sex relationships and marriages are morally wrong. Will Evelyn focus on Patty's ability to produce as a vice president or will she get stuck on Patty's primary dimension of diversity? Will Evelyn allow her personal beliefs to interfere with professional workplace behaviors?

The ability to "see past" the primary dimensions of diversity is an important skill to master for an individual to truly *be diversity competent.* It is through acknowledging and recognizing the primary dimensions of diversity that individuals can gain access to the secondary dimensions of diversity others possess. When dealing with the primary characteristics of an individual, you may find that she or he does not look like you with regards to age, body orientation, ethnicity, race, sexual orientation and gender. Even so, you may need to acknowledge and recognize that these characteristics exist and move on to learning about the individual's secondary dimensions of diversity.

On a similar note, Loden and Rosener define the secondary dimensions of diversity as, *"Those that can be changed. They are mutable differences that we acquire, discard and/or modify throughout our lives."* The secondary dimensions of diversity are those that are most often acquired during life experiences and circumstances. Many of them are gained through events and experiences beyond our childhood years. When individuals and organizations truly embrace a person's secondary dimensions of diversity, this is the beginning of a sustainable and long-lasting personal and professional relationship.

When individuals move from the primary dimensions of diversity to the secondary dimensions of diversity, true, real, sincere and authentic relationship building begins. At this point, individuals are able to engage in honest communication, difficult dialogue and deep discussion regarding diversity issues. For true relationships to begin, the secondary dimensions of diversity including personal values, religious and spiritual beliefs, education level, culture and basic interests and hobbies offer common ground. To fully understand another person's deep-seated values, individuals must have sustained interactions with one another over a significant period of time. Consequently, once you no longer see primary dimensions of diversity as barriers, a whole world of dialogue opens up between you and the other person. You are then able to *ask* about their beliefs, culture, family, politics and other pertinent information. You can *find out* if you share any similar hobbies, and you can begin to develop a relationship with that person based on who they are as an individual.

> "In the end, antiblack, antifemale, and all forms of discrimination are equivalent to the same thing—antihumanism.
> **Shirley Chisholm**

Don't Judge a Book by its Cover: The Jon Lauer Story

It was Sunday, but not your ordinary Sunday. It was the last day I would officially live at home with my mother and siblings; it was a beautiful warm summer day in August. The year was 1989 and I was 17 years young. I had finished packing and loading my 1978 baby blue two-door Chevy Cutlass Supreme and was heading off to college. I had chosen to attend a school in the Chicago land area, Elmhurst College–a school in a predominately white city that was 45-minutes from the west side of Chicago where I was born, bred and raised.

Later that afternoon, after settling into my small dorm room, a guy I had spotted in the room across the hall from me knocked on the door. Extending a friendly hand, he introduced himself, saying, "Hi, I'm Jon Lauer. I'm from Sheboygan, Wisconsin."

Although I was suspicious of his intent and guarded emotionally, I replied, "I'm Jermaine Davis. I'm from the west side of Chicago." I analyzed Jon's body language from head to toe.

Jon replied, wearing a friendly, welcoming and wide Kool-Aid smile from ear to ear, "I would like to meet a few friends before classes begin on Wednesday, and I noticed you moving in earlier, so I thought I would come over and introduce myself to you because we live across the hall from one another."

I hesitated and reflected on my Uncle Ricky's words, "The white man is *scaandalous*." These words were playing over and over in my mind like a CD stuck on repeat. My thoughts continued to when Uncle Ricky would add, "The white man is out to get one over on us. Look at what they did to the Native Americans! They stole their land from them! They even mistreat their own white women by oppressing and suppressing them! Hell, women didn't even get the right to vote until 1920. And, don't forget we never got our forty acres and a mule that they promised to the black man after slavery!" He'd continue, "Jermaine, black people built America and it was all free labor that built the United *Snakes* of America. Now, tell me how do you justify those kinds of atrocities and then go to church and pray to a Christian God! I don't understand it, man."

Still staring at Jon, Uncle Ricky's warnings made me mute as I stood silent, unable to reply, wondering, *what does this white dude really want with me?*

Two days later, I was dribbling my basketball in front of the residence hall, enjoying a little exercise. From out of nowhere, Jon appeared again and asked if I would like to join him in a game of horse or one-on-one. I wanted to shoot some hoops with him, but instead of saying, "Yes," I heard Uncle Ricky's lingering and infectious words over and over again maneuvering my thoughts and feelings. I rapidly muttered, "No thanks. I'm cool, man." I was not rude, but cautious.

A few days later, Jon stopped by again. This time he asked if I would like to go with him to see a comedian appearing on campus at the college union. Again, though I really wanted to say, "Yes," I once again gave into my internal dialogue and decided not to hang out with Jon and his friends who were all white females and males.

Later, Jon offered to share a care package filled with popcorn, chips, fruit roll-ups, pop-tarts, trail mix, assorted nuts and sugarless chewing gum, with me. *I thought to myself, my mother hasn't sent me anything, and this guy has all these goodies and he's sharing his goodies with me...a guy who I had regularly turned down despite his friendly overtures.* Then with the smell of those goodies lingering in my nostrils, I began to think rationally and not emotionally. I reasoned that Uncle Ricky might be grossly wrong regarding the white man being "the Devil manifested in the flesh." I began to think that if Jon is a devil, he sure is a good one because he is personable, pleasant and persistent.

My Life-Changing Diversity *Ah-Ha* Moment

My experience with Jon Lauer was my first and major, diversity *Ah-Ha* moment. It was like a great mental, emotional and spiritual awakening. I finally had the courage to challenge, dispute and refute my uncle's dangerous and poisonous diversity-related advice. I was now thinking independently and freely, developing my own ideals and philosophies regarding diversity and race relations.

Suddenly, my motivations for not responding to Jon's friendly overtures were unimportant. Though Jon had done nothing to violate or disrespect me personally, I persisted in judging him as a potentially dangerous white man instead of as Jon Lauer, an individual who just *happened* to be a white man. I was prejudging Jon based on my Uncle Ricky's tainted perceptions and negative diversity encounter that he had experienced and intentionally passed on to me. Initially, I saw Jon as a white guy...the kind that Uncle Ricky had vehemently warned me to be careful of. By deliberately and aggressively recognizing and challenging my Diversity BAPS (Biases, Assumptions, Prejudices and Stereotypes), the two of us became great friends, playing basketball, hanging out and studying together. In fact, during our junior year, the two of us traveled to Lexington, Kentucky, to participate in a Habitat for Humanity homebuilding initiative for low-income families.

Diversity Conflict and Tension

In my book, *Leading with Greatness*, I explain the root cause of conflict by stating, ***"All conflict is the result of an unmet or violated need, want or expectation."*** Human beings verbally and/or physically attack one another when they feel or perceive their basic needs, wants and expectations are being avoided, denied, minimized or ignored. Every human being is entitled to basic civil and human rights in their private, personal and professional life. When these basic civil and human rights are unmet or violated, you will experience diversity conflict and tension within your organization or school.

I believe everyone–and I mean everyone–deserves to have her or his basic civil and human rights respected and honored. When individuals communicate their wants and expectations, these variables can often and will often lead to philosophical debates within organizations because some wants and expectations are perceived as "too unrealistic." My goal here is not to provide a canned or one size fits all answer, but to get individuals and organizations to understand that a diversity-friendly, inclusive and welcoming environment can only be constructed and cultivated when diverse communities feel and perceive their diverse needs, wants and expectations are just as important as the dominant culture or group.

Why do most people avoid diversity conflict and tension? It is because they are afraid of and feel uncomfortable addressing diversity issues. Some excuses they may give include:

• "It's awkward and stressful addressing diversity issues."

• "I don't want to hurt anyone's feelings or say the wrong thing."

• "I just don't know what to do or say."

You will be one step closer to resolving diversity conflict and tension constructively when you learn and understand why individuals and organizations often deal with diversity conflict and tension destructively.

The goal is to reduce, if not eliminate, diversity conflict and tension; however, one may ask, How do you go about reducing and eliminating diversity conflict and tension? Remember, people strike out at one another when their basic civil and human rights are being avoided, denied, minimized and ignored. Ask yourself two questions as an individual or organization: (1) am I preventing others from experiencing their basic civil and human rights and (2) what do I need to do on a daily basis to ensure that people are being treated justly, equitably and fairly?

So what is happening when individuals and organizations avoid and ignore diversity conflict and tension? They are attempting to prevent themselves from experiencing diversity stress. What is stress? *Stress is any situation that individuals perceive as threatening to their healthy mental, emotional and physical well-being.* Diversity conflict and tension issues can really elevate an individual's stress level, threatening and disturbing the person's mental, emotional and physical harmony. Diversity stress takes place when individuals or leaders who are conflict-avoidant have to deal with inappropriate comments and unprofessional behaviors in the workplace or school settings. Avoiding and ignoring diversity conflict and tension only leads to and creates more diversity conflict and tension.

The Three Nasty Evils of Diversity Conflict

It is important to recognize that diversity incompetence is present in all individuals and organizations. There are degrees of inability or unwillingness to communicate across differences. The key to reducing and eliminating diversity conflict and tension is to first identify which nasty evil of diversity conflict is potentially plaguing, destroying and preventing you or your organization from being diversity competent. The Three Nasty Evils of Diversity Conflict include: (1) Diversity Avoidance, (2) Diversity Denial and (3) Diversity Minimization.

(1) Nasty Evil of Diversity Conflict - Diversity Avoidance

Diversity avoidance occurs when individuals and organizations mentally, emotionally and physically ignore and stay away from diversity conflict and tension. They know diversity conflict and tension exists, but they refuse to address, confront and deal with it. The goal of the avoider is to avoid the stress that accompanies diversity conflict and tension. Avoiding diversity problems may keep organizations stress-free for awhile, but the issues consistently resurface, leading to unhappy and unsatisfied personal and professional relationships. *Diversity avoidance is an intentional decision to ignore diversity concerns and issues rather than handling them constructively and proactively.* When leaders of organizations avoid diversity conflict and tension, the entire organization suffers.

Tips for Handling Diversity Avoidance

- Help the individual reduce her or his diversity anxiety. This means being up front about the diversity issues that exist and helping she or he understand why the avoidance is happening in the first place. Most people avoid issues that bring discomfort. Help them identify their diversity discomfort with this question: Is it a mental, emotional or physical discomfort or all three? Helping them to pinpoint the cause of their diversity discomfort is instrumental in helping them to overcome diversity conflict and tension. Once they identify their specific diversity discomfort, they can generate ideas and strategies specific to the organization and address the key diversity issues. This process requires honest communication and open dialogue.

- Show them the benefits of addressing and confronting diversity conflict and tension. Communicate to the individual how much more effective, efficient and productive things will be within the organization when diversity conflict and tension is handled constructively and proactively.

- Show them the liabilities of not addressing and confronting diversity conflict and tension. Communicate to them the possibilities of lawsuits, employee and student disengagement and turnover and increased diversity conflict and tension that may occur because the diversity problems are being avoided and ignored.

- Help the individual develop an optimistic paradigm for resolving diversity conflict and tension. This may involve showing optimism for conflict resolution and showing them the combined benefits of addressing the diversity concerns and issues. Unfortunately, when people think of conflict, thoughts of pessimism are more prevalent than optimism. If you can show individuals the benefits despite the challenges, you will increase your chances of buy-in to achieve maximum results.

(2) Nasty Evil of Diversity Conflict - Diversity Denial

Diversity denial occurs when individuals and organizations deliberately refuse to acknowledge, admit or recognize the presence of diversity conflict and tension. When colleagues, employees and students share their diversity concerns, their concerns are immediately dismissed, shot down or totally rejected. People in diversity denial refuse to acknowledge and recognize diversity conflict and tension even when presented with facts, figures and documented experiences that are both valid and substantiated. These individuals refuse to allow diversity conflict and tension to register on their diversity radar screen.

Tips for Handling Diversity Denial

- Provide them with documented and factual diversity-related conflicts and experiences that are presently occurring. It may be difficult, but remember to show more facts than emotion. If you show more emotion, you may derail the message you are trying to convey because emotional expression can easily distract individuals who are more cerebral, impersonal and pragmatic.

  The more factual you can be at communicating diversity conflict and tension you see happening, the easier it will be for the individual to be less defensive. This is best understood by using an example we discussed earlier. If you work at a grocery store, and you feel your manager is in diversity denial about ordering more diverse products, you could present her or him with data on what the current demographics are within your community. In other words, *who* is your customer?

- Explain to them how it makes you feel when your diversity concerns and issues *are* acknowledged, recognized and seen as valid. This approach is an emotional appeal that may or may not go over well, but your goal is to connect how feeling valued and respected as a human being will increase your effectiveness and productivity as a colleague, employee or student.

Show them the liabilities of not addressing and confronting diversity conflict and tension. This relates to diversity avoidance as well. Denying the problem can lead to increased diversity conflict and tension and possibly to legal action if the diversity issues are continuously denied and rejected.

(3) Nasty Evil of Diversity Conflict - Diversity Minimization

Diversity minimization occurs when individuals and organizations reduce diversity conflict and tension to the smallest possible size. This reduction of critical concerns and issues is done very skillfully through the use of manipulation. The goal is to make diversity conflict and tension as insignificant and as unimportant as possible. Diversity Minimizers are the queens and kings of downplaying diversity conflict and tension. If a Diversity Minimizer can convince you that your diversity conflict and tension is minute, irrelevant or blown out of proportion, then she or he knows you will not expect them to take action on such an insignificant matter. This can be particularly dangerous if the Diversity Minimizer is in a position of influence within your organization. Be extremely careful of those who are persuasive, influential and witty with word play because they are more likely to convince you to put your critical diversity concerns and issues on the back burner. Once they are put on the back burner, they will most likely not be addressed, leaving you feeling cheated, deceived, walked over and disengaged as a colleague, employee or student.

Tips for Handling Diversity Minimization

- Explain to the Diversity Minimizer how you feel when your diversity concerns and issues are not heard, seen, recognized and understood as significant. This may appeal to their emotions and they may begin to understand that your diversity concerns and issues are more important than they perceived.

- Explain to them how the organization's diversity conflict and tension has affected you personally and professionally. This will appeal to the individual's logic as well as to her or his emotions. The person may begin to see that what they see as minimal and insignificant and, in fact, a serious diversity issue to others. Appeal to their rational mind by showing them how the present diversity climate and environment is counterproductive for the organization or school.

- Ask them what is preventing them from recognizing and understanding the severity of your diversity concerns and issues. Do not ask this question immediately because the person will more than likely become personally and professionally defensive. When they see you as a human being and the issue is important to you (and others), they may be more able to see how the diversity problem is affecting you and them on a deeper level. Use the "power of the pause" to allow the individual to carefully answer your diversity concerns and issues.

■   ■   ■

Part 2

**Diversity
Competence
Defined**

G enerally speaking, a competent person is an individual who is able to consistently perform above average on the task at hand using a skill set acquired through education, experience and training. Competent women and men supersede mediocrity when performing a task. They are effective at whatever they do because they accomplish and achieve their desired results often. In this vein, *diversity competence is the willingness and ability to communicate effectively across differences through understanding the differences of others.*

Understanding Culture and Cultural Differences

To communicate and interact effectively across differences, it is imperative for individuals and organizations to understand the culture and subculture of the individuals with whom they are attempting to build cultural bridges and diversity alliances with. Currently as a college professor and previously as a marketing and sales representative, I have learned you cannot market or sell to specific diverse groups or populations until you learn two important aspects regarding them: (1) their individuality (personal identity) and (2) their cultural background.

So what is culture? *Culture is a way of life shared by a group of people, where beliefs, customary practices and patterns are passed down from generation to generation.* People who have similarities in the type of food they eat, their belief system, languages(s) they speak, traditions they honor, attire they wear and festivities they celebrate. Cultural programming is so powerful that it conditions individuals within a given culture on what to value and what not to value, what is good and what is bad, what is safe and what is unsafe, what is positive and what is negative, what is acceptable and what is unacceptable and how to behave and how not to behave.

Culture shapes the way people see the world. Yes, culture shapes an individual's worldview as well as how they analyze, process and interpret diverse encounters and experiences. All cultures, and I mean ALL cultures have their own way of looking at and making sense of the world. This attitudinal belief and practice is known as ethnocentrism. *Ethnocentrism occurs when diversity conflict and tension arise because one culture feels as if its cultural perspective, worldview*

***and diversity interpretations are far better, greater and superior than other
cultures and diverse groups.***

Ronald Alder, Russel Proctor and Neil Towne give an excellent example of cultural
differences and perceptual differences in their book *Looking Out Looking In* when
they write:

> *"The range of cultural differences is wide. Even beliefs about
> the very value of talk differ from one culture to another. Western
> cultures view talk as desirable and use it for social purposes as
> well as for task performance. Silence has a negative value in
> these cultures. It is likely to be interpreted as lack of interest,
> unwillingness to communicate, hostility, anxiety, shyness, or a sign
> of interpersonal incompatibility. Westerners are uncomfortable
> with silence, which they find embarrassing and awkward.*
>
> *On the other hand, Asian cultures perceive talk differently.
> For thousands of years, Asian cultures have discouraged the
> expression of thoughts and feelings. Silence is valued, as Taoist
> sayings indicate: 'In much talk there is great weariness,' or 'One
> who speaks does not know; one who knows does not speak.'
> Unlike most North Americans who are uncomfortable with
> silence, Japanese and Chinese people believe that remaining
> quiet is the proper state when there is nothing to be said. In
> Asian cultures, a talkative person is often considered a show-off
> or insincere."*

One key component to remember regarding cultural programming is that cultural
practices and customs do not always determine or predict how individuals born or
raised in a particular culture will behave or communicate. Most often, people
make dangerous and incorrect predictions about how all people of a particular
cultural group will behave based on cultural and traditional customs and practices.
Cultural customs, patterns, practices and traditions only provide a foundational
premise of how individuals of a particular culture or diverse group will behave or
communicate. The philosophy and practice of diversity competence encourages
and implies that getting to know individuals *personally* is the most effective and

respectful way to build cultural bridges and diversity alliances.

We all live within the confines of one or more cultures. Other cultures can be in accordance with our own or vastly discordant with our cultural beliefs and practices. Diversity competence is acknowledging that culture shapes everyone, including you, and that understanding cultural differences can and will lead to minimizing cultural clashes. Again, agreement with another culture is not a requirement of being diversity competent. However, understanding diverse people and cultures is critical to conflict resolution. Taking the quality time to understand the beliefs, customs and practices of other cultures goes a long way toward reducing diversity collisions and ethnocentrism.

Being diversity competent involves learning new patterns of thinking, feeling, behaving and communicating. It requires that you appropriately and effectively apply these diversity competent skills when interacting with those different from you. It does not mean you need to give up or nullify your own beliefs although you may decide to divorce certain diversity beliefs you once were married to due to faulty thinking or inaccurate information. Nor does it mean you give up any sense of personal or cultural pride, which helps define you personally. Rather, it signifies your continuing education while acquiring diversity knowledge such as beliefs, values and cultural practices of those who are different from you.

Additionally, being diversity competent can be regarded as having the "get along" factor and skill set. It implies a willingness to see the differences and similarities among people yet recognizing that the real objective is communicating effectively and getting along with diverse people despite their unique differences. Diversity competent individuals and organizations ask and answer the diversity question: What are the best and most effective communication strategies to employ or eliminate with regard to reducing diversity conflict and tension?

The journey of diversity competence begins with eradicating the notion and emotions of guilt and shame for not being diversity competent as an individual or organization. I believe the greatest shame is when individuals and organizations blatantly decide to be diversity incompetent. Being diversity competent does not mean you know every diversity fact, figure or statistic, nor does it mean you are versed in every culture and can speak all languages and clearly understand all accents and dialects. Any balanced individual who maintains a healthy private, personal and professional life cannot and will not have the time to know about every diverse population, issue or topic. However, I do suggest for starters that you spend time doing your diversity homework regarding the communities, issues and topics you face frequently where you work, live, shop and play.

> "Being diversity competent involves learning new patterns of thinking, feeling, behaving and communicating."
> **Jermaine M. Davis**

Diversity competence does imply that learning about diverse communities, issues and topics is a life-long education, journey and exploration for all individuals and organizations that are seriously committed to getting along with and communicating effectively across differences through understanding the differences of others. Developing diversity competence becomes much easier when individuals and organizations accept and embrace that there are basic human and civil rights inherent to all individuals. Even the late Thomas Jefferson wrote of equality and human rights between June 11 and June 28, 1776, in the Declaration of Independence when he penned:

> *"We hold these truths to be self-evident, that all Men are created equal, that they are endowed by their Creator with certain unalienable Rights, that among these are Life, Liberty, and the Pursuit of Happiness."*

The concept of basic human and civil rights is often spoken of as the "ideal truth;" it is less often put into practice when dealing with people who are not "the same" as we are or whose diversity we may not like or feel comfortable with. If individuals are perceived as too different or radically different from the norm, they are typically denied their life, their liberty and their pursuit of happiness. Now you may be asking yourself, "Who holds the power to deny certain groups their basic human and civil rights?" Typically, American society has labeled heterosexuals, men, the wealthy, European Americans and Christians as the dominant and privileged groups. The dominant and privileged groups are individuals of a group who receive unearned benefits and opportunities due to their group membership; they hold the power most often to define and determine what is "acceptable" or "unacceptable," "normal" or "abnormal," "just" or "unjust" and "right or "wrong."

Their beliefs, concerns and issues are automatically regarded as the norm and taken into consideration most often within American institutions, corporations and schools. Typically, America has labeled members of the GLBT community, women, the poor, people of color and those who have religious and spiritual practices other than Christianity as oppressed groups. Quite simply, they are not part of the dominant culture or privileged group. This paradigm is very controversial and divisive because many do not believe we live in a dichotomized America.

American society has a long history of separation, such as the rich and the poor, the haves and the have nots, separate but equal, blacks and whites, natives and immigrants and Christianity and Judaism and more recently, Islam. This denial of access and opportunity happens intentionally and unintentionally, covertly and overtly, blatantly and clandestinely. However, if you subscribe to the ideal that we are all entitled to basic human and civil rights no matter our diversity, the philosophy and practice of diversity competence should be easily accepted and embraced. Disenfranchised, oppressed and marginalized group members are not asking for special rights, but the same rights that every American citizen enjoys.

It is a fallacy to believe that you will become diversity competent with every diverse community or diverse population. Once again, how could you, and when would you have the time? Rather, I suggest focusing your diversity efforts and energies on initially understanding the populations of those you most often encounter in life, school and work. You will use this as your foundation for building diversity competence. In addition, you may choose to focus on diverse groups who you find yourself struggling with or the diverse communities you cannot form an opinion about because you know nothing or very little about their diversity and cultural background. Yes, being diversity competent involves time, work and effort. It is a life-long commitment and an ongoing educational process.

Remember that seeking and having an *understanding* about a certain cultural group or diverse community does not mean you need to agree with all they practice. There will be times when you may not agree with an ethnic group's cultural practices and rituals. It is important to seek first to understand the cultural practices and rituals before passing judgment. The process of seeking to understand is an act of respect,

kindness and interpersonal cooperation. It is easy to
practice ethnocentrism when we disagree with a
culturally diverse group's way of life. The practice of
ethnocentrism is arrogant, and arrogance interferes
with good communication and leads to diversity
conflict and tension. Being diversity competent

> "Communication is
> the beginning of
> understanding."
> **Sara Cooper**

means you know enough about a particular cultural group or diverse community
to comfortably communicate and interact with those who are different from you.

In many ways, your potential as a future employee, colleague, teacher or salesperson
could depend on your diversity competent skills. Your ability to interact and work
among diverse people, live among diverse people or teach diverse people has
become a skill set employers look for when hiring new employees. This is true
especially if your personal and professional work involves human interaction,
whether that is through e-mail, telephone or face-to-face communication.

Moving from Diversity Incompetence
to Diversity Competence

So what exactly is diversity incompetence? *Diversity incompetence is the
unwillingness and/or inability to communicate effectively across differences.*
Some individuals and organizations are diversity incompetent because they simply
lack the three fundamental skills of diversity competence: attitudinal skills,
behavioral skills and communicative skills (I will cover these skills in part four).
These fundamental skills are requirements for individuals and organizations that
need and desire to communicate effectively with their diverse clients, colleagues,
customers, employees and students. I have learned over the last ten years from
teaching college adults, conducting diversity trainings across the country and from
researching diversity literature that there are six core reasons why individuals
and organizations lack the ability to communicate effectively across differences.
These six core reasons include (these will be covered later in the book):

(1) Diversity Anxiety and Uncertainty
(2) Fear of the Unknown
(3) Cultural Ignorance

(4) Lack of Diversity Education
(5) Lack of Diversity Experience
(6) Lack of Diversity Exposure

I have witnessed and heard countless stories from grade school students to high-ranking executives that one or more of these core reasons have personally immobilized or paralyzed individuals and organizations from extending themselves to individuals who are different from them or the dominant group or culture.

Some individuals and organizations are diversity incompetent because they deliberately and intentionally refuse to learn how *not* to communicate effectively across differences. In other words, as the definition suggests, they are unwilling to be diversity competent even if it negatively affects their clients, colleagues, customers, employees and students. I have also learned from teaching at some of the largest colleges and universities in Minnesota and from conducting diversity workshops on major college campuses, social service organizations, government agencies and small to large corporations that there are four core reasons why individuals and some organizations are unwilling to learn how to communicate effectively across differences.

These four core reasons include:

(1) Diversity Apathy
(2) Diversity Cynicism
(3) Diversity Intolerance
(4) Ethnocentrism and Arrogance

These four self-imposed barriers remind me of a quote by Civil Rights activist and author, James Baldwin when he writes, "Not everything that is faced can be changed, but nothing can be changed until it is faced." The latter part of Mr. Baldwin's quote deeply explains why so much diversity chaos, conflict and tension still exist in many corporations, communities and schools today. This is because of unwilling individuals who refuse to acknowledge, accept, embrace and deal with the reality of a diverse society.

To fully embrace the philosophy and practice of diversity competence, individuals and organizations must commit to and be willing to experience a cultural paradigm shift. The philosophy and practice of diversity competence does not ask individuals and organizations to change their diversity attitudes, behaviors and communication styles without them first understanding and seeing the benefits of diversity competence. It is imperative to understand why you are making the diversity shift before you can fully commit and dedicate yourself and your organization to diversity competence. Ask yourself:

- What are the short-term and long-term benefits of making a shift in my diversity attitude, behaviors and interpersonal interactions?

- How appreciative will your colleagues, clients, customers, employees and students be? Explain your answer.

- How will diversity competence or diversity incompetence affect your organization and your businesses' bottom-line profits?

- What are the personal and professional liabilities of not implementing the philosophy and practice of diversity competence?

Becoming Diversity Competent

When people ask me, "Jermaine, what does it take for an individual or organization to become diversity competent?" I reply, "To be diversity competent, individuals and organizations must become proficient in the areas of attitudinal diversity, behavioral diversity and communicative diversity." Don't worry…I have dedicated part four of *Be Diversity Competent* to exploring in detail the three core skills of the philosophy and practice of diversity competence. Many of my clients tell me that they are confused, frustrated and perplexed with regard to how to best go about creating a diversity-friendly, inclusive and welcoming workplace or school environment for their clients, colleagues, customers, employees and students.

> "Not everything that is faced can be changed, but nothing can be changed until it is faced."
> **James Baldwin**

As a professional keynote speaker and workshop leader, I want to be completely honest with you by stating, "You cannot rush the process of becoming diversity competent." Diversity competence is a gradual process and life-long education that requires full commitment, relentless dedication and constant education and practice. You will mess up at times during the process and, I repeat, you *will* mess up at times during the process of becoming diversity competent.

The Four Pillars of Diversity Competence

It is important to understand that becoming diversity competent is a gradual and life-long educational process. Before an individual or organization can become proficient in the diversity areas of attitudinal skills, behavioral skills and communicative skills, they must first embrace the four pillars of diversity competence. The four pillars of diversity competence are: (1) Diversity Will, (2) Diversity Desire, (3) Diversity Knowledge and (4) Diversity Skill.

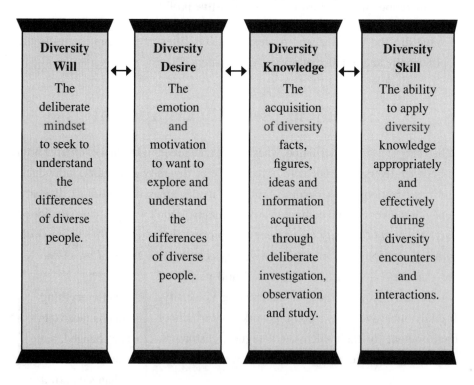

Diversity Will		**Diversity Desire**		**Diversity Knowledge**		**Diversity Skill**
The deliberate mindset to seek to understand the differences of diverse people.	↔	The emotion and motivation to want to explore and understand the differences of diverse people.	↔	The acquisition of diversity facts, figures, ideas and information acquired through deliberate investigation, observation and study.	↔	The ability to apply diversity knowledge appropriately and effectively during diversity encounters and interactions.

The following scenario incorporates the four pillars of diversity competence. It illustrates how each pillar is critical to fully understanding and embracing the philosophy and practice of diversity competence.

Exploring and Understanding Different Dimensions of Diversity

This scenario provides you with a framework for developing an overall paradigm to becoming diversity competent by using the four pillars of diversity competence.

The Four Pillars of Diversity Competence in Practice

Kyle is a 57-year–old-white male, Catholic, a veteran and life-long resident of a rural police force. Kyle was recently assigned to partner with a rookie officer named Kelly who is about half Kyle's age, African-American, lesbian and from the inner city. Let us assume that both Kelly and Kyle have very limited diversity experience with each other's different dimensions of diversity. How does each officer begin to develop diversity competence in this workplace situation?

There are seven different dimensions of diversity that distinguish Kelly and Kyle's uniqueness from one another. Their differences do not have to lead to diversity conflict and tension; however, the laws of probability teach us that the more people are different from one another, the greater the chances of diversity conflict and tension. The best defense for Kelly and Kyle is regular communication and developing a sense of understanding for one another's unique backgrounds to reduce, if not completely eliminate, diversity conflict and tension.

Here is a breakdown of the dimensions of diversity that distinguish Kelly from Kyle:

Kelly's Diversity	Kyle's Diversity
African-American	White
Female	Male
Lesbian	Heterosexual
Generation X	Baby Boomer
Spiritual	Catholic
Inner-City (Urban) Lifestyle	Rural Lifestyle
Rookie Police Officer	Veteran Police Officer

Diversity Will

Certainly Kelly and Kyle can "run" from the diversity encounter, request a change of partners or avoid and ignore their new diverse partner altogether. Alternatively, their diversity competence journey could begin with understanding diversity competence pillar #1, which is being open-minded enough to develop a diversity will. ***Diversity will is the deliberate mindset to seek to understand the differences of diverse people.*** In this scenario, Kelly and Kyle must consciously and intentionally make a mental commitment to pursue and embrace this new diversity opportunity. Each officer must deliberately make up her or his mind to learn more about one another despite their diversity anxiety, fear and uncertainty.

So will each officer initially have some sort of diversity anxiety, fear and uncertainty? Absolutely! Does possessing diversity anxiety, fear and uncertainty make Kelly and Kyle bad individuals? Absolutely not! It *does* mean that the veteran and rookie officer must make a commitment to doing their diversity homework to truly understand each other's different dimensions of diversity if she or he wants to communicate effectively on a personal and professional level.

Diversity competence in this scenario would involve a deliberate and intentional commitment on Kelly and Kyle's part to fully embrace the new diversity challenge set before them, and each of them must be willing to allow diversity into their personal and professional lives. Diversity competence requires individuals and organizations to be willing and open-minded enough to give diversity a fair chance without judgment. Getting to know a stranger and feeling comfortable with a partner with such different primary dimensions of diversity as you have, will take commitment, action and courage. For diversity bridges to be built and established in the workplace, each partner must be as willing and open-minded enough to make diversity work despite potential diversity conflict and tension.

How can Kelly and Kyle get to know one another better on a personal and professional level? A technique they can use is the DALO Approach. The DALO Approach (outlined below) is an interpersonal communication tool I developed and first wrote about in my book *Leading with Greatness*. The DALO Approach is designed to help individuals and leaders within all types of organizations to learn more about the individuals they are communicating, interacting and working with on a regular basis. The DALO Approach can significantly reduce if not totally eliminate diversity anxiety, fear and uncertainty if used appropriately and effectively.

The DALO Approach is an acronym, which stands for:

The DALO Approach

Dialogue – A dialogue is an honest and open conversation where there is an exchange of diverse ideas and perspectives.

Asking Questions – The respectful process of gaining and gathering information about others to enhance and improve personal and professional interactions.

Listen – The process of hearing, honoring, respecting and understanding diverse people's experiences and stories without interruption.

Observe – The process of paying close attention to individuals' personal and professional concerns, hobbies, interests and issues.

To reduce diversity discomfort, Kelly and Kyle must commit to and practice dialoguing (**D**) with one another without judgment to learn more about one another's beliefs, cultural practices, ethics, morals, preferences and values. They must engage in asking (**A**) respectful personal and professional questions to get more acquainted with one another; it is imperative that they listen deeply to each other's worldview and perspective. Remember, listening does not mean agreement. ***Deep listening (L) means you listen without interruption until you fully understand the other person's ideas and perspectives.*** Successful deep listening occurs when the communicator is completely convinced the listener fully understands their intended message. Deep listening around controversial diversity issues is a critical factor to resolving diversity conflict and tension.

Many people misconstrue what understanding means. Understanding an individual from her or his viewpoint does not mean you have to agree with them. Although you may totally agree with them, fully understanding a person's perspective implies you comprehend the message or messages they are attempting to convey. Remember, every human being wants to feel like she or he matters, and two of the strongest ways to communicate to someone that she or he matters is by *listening* to and *understanding* where they are coming from. By this I mean *deeply* listening to their voice and their voice of experience (their life experiences as well as their diversity experiences). One of the quickest and surest ways to devalue another human being is to *not* listen to them and to demean, disregard and disrespect their life experiences. You can discover and find out a great deal about other people by simply practicing the art of deep listening without interruption.

Finally, Kelly and Kyle can get to know one another better while reducing their diversity anxiety, fear and uncertainty through observation. Observation (**O**) means Kelly and Kyle are paying close attention to one another's surroundings – their office cubicle and decorations, clothing they wear, mannerisms and reactions, books and magazines they read, jewelry they wear, topics they discuss or do not discuss and personal and professional hobbies and interests. Observation does not mean you are being noisy or intrusive; it implies you are paying close attention to what matters most to the people you communicate, interact and work with. It increases your chances of making a diversity connection as well as finding out and discovering commonalities, likenesses and similarities you both share.

Diversity Desire

After Kelly and Kyle develop and practice their new philosophy of diversity competence by seeking to learn and understand more about each others' differences, they must cultivate diversity pillar #2, which is diversity desire. ***Diversity desire is the emotion and motivation to want to explore and understand the differences of diverse people.*** Ralph Waldo Emerson once stated, "Nothing great was ever achieved without enthusiasm." To achieve diversity competence, individuals and organizations must be enthusiastic about their diversity journey and exploration of welcoming new individuals and cultures. Diversity desire requires individuals and organizations to be open-minded.

I often hear people tenaciously expressing ideas of changing their organization or school, or they want to change the world, but rarely do I hear individuals talking about changing themselves. Our society, organizations and schools will change when we decide to change as *individuals.* Henry David Thoreau reinforces my perspective when he writes, "Things do not change: we change." And of course the classic Mahatma Gandhi quote encourages personal accountability regarding making the world a better place when he writes, "You must be the change you seek in the world."

With that said, I know some people will never cultivate a desire for diversity concerns, issues and topics. However, the philosophy and practice of diversity competence teaches that individuals and organizations must cultivate and develop a diversity desire to improve diversity relations within our communities, corporations, houses of faith and worship and schools.

Diversity proponents are proactive about learning about diverse people when new dimensions of diversity become a part of their community, organizations, houses of faith and worship and schools. They are cheerleaders for justice, equality and inclusion. Diversity proponents zealously seek to explore, listen to and understand the unique differences of diverse people. I am not really concerned about diversity proponents because they are typically eager and emotionally motivated to want to learn more about the differences of diverse people.

My real concern is what I refer to as the diversity *opponents* and the diversity "*I don't knows.*" It is quite evident where the diversity opponents' stand, but the diversity "*I don't knows*" are typically indecisive or undecided regarding where they stand on diversity issues and topics. If Kelly and Kyle are either diversity opponents or diversity "*I don't knows,*" then it becomes difficult for either one of them to cultivate and develop a desire to fully become diversity competent. In either case, you will see a

> "Change is
> inevitable,
> growth is
> optional."
> **Unknown**

resistance to diversity communication either passively, aggressively or passive-aggressively. Cultivating and developing a desire for diversity cannot be coerced, mandated or legislated; it can only be strongly encouraged. However, individuals and organizations can begin the process of cultivating and developing a desire for diversity by learning to see the advantages and benefits of diversity.

If analyzing the benefits of becoming diversity competent is not motivation enough for individuals and organizations or if the civil, human and moral cases are not compelling enough, I would ask that they look at and tally the cost of being diversity incompetent. I would ask individuals and organizations to study the disadvantages and liabilities of being diversity incompetent. Unfortunately, many times individuals and organizations are motivated to explore and take action when pain and pressure forces them to take action. Now, some may take bitter action while others will become proactive after a painful wake-up call. I often ask workshop participants, "How much is diversity incompetence costing you and your organization personally, professionally, legally and financially?" and "How is your personal and organizational reputation being communicated internally and externally as a result of diversity competence or diversity incompetence?"

As stated earlier, I am a realist regarding diversity issues, which means I know that there will never, ever be a 100% buy-in for the philosophy and practice of diversity competence. However, the idealistic side of me encourages, motivates and compels me to continue my diversity teaching, writing and workshops because I know for a fact that there are individuals and organizations that desperately desire to move from diversity incompetence to diversity competence, both personally and professionally.

Even after Kelly and Kyle are willing to embrace and develop the first two pillars of diversity competence, diversity will and diversity desire, they are only half prepared to begin the process of becoming diversity competent. Although they are both mentally and emotionally prepared to embark upon a diversity quest, they are still lacking the other two pillars of diversity competence. Now, for Kelly and Kyle to work together cohesively and collaboratively while respecting each others' different dimensions of diversity, they must proactively and intentionally gather diversity knowledge of each other, which is pillar #3.

Diversity Knowledge

Diversity knowledge is the acquisition of diversity facts, figures, ideas and information acquired through deliberate investigation, observation and study. I call the process of acquiring diversity knowledge doing your diversity homework or doing your diversity due diligence. I am very honest and upfront with individuals and organizations regarding the process of becoming diversity competent. Honestly, diversity work requires time, energy and effort, just like any other skill in which someone seeks to develop proficiency.

I often find that many individuals and organizations only pay lip service to the philosophy and practice of diversity competence. They say they want to improve customer relations, client relations, employee relations and student relations, but their diversity actions, commitment and dedication are far from what they actually do. No one, and I repeat, no one, can become competent or proficient in any skill or area if they will not commit and dedicate herself or himself to the task or initiative requiring their undivided attention. Diversity homework, diversity due diligence and diversity dues must be willingly paid prior to diversity competence and skill proficiency.

I will often conduct the following exercise when I give keynotes and workshops on my book, *Get Up Off Your Butt & Do It NOW! Staying Motivated Even When You Don't Feel Like It.* I ask individuals and organizations to identify one individual, team or organizational goal they would like to accomplish in the next three to six months. Once they have identified that goal, I ask that they write the goal down on their handout or inside their personal journal. I then proceed to ask the audience members to stare at the goal for two minutes and recite the goal to themselves silently seven times before the two minutes are up. After the exercise, I ask everyone to look up, and I then proceed to ask two of my favorite goal achievement and goal attainment questions: "How much does your goal cost you?" and "What price are you willing to pay to achieve your dream, goal and aspiration?"

> "In the end, we will not remember the words of
> our enemies, but the silence of our friends."
> **Dr. Martin Luther King, Jr.**

If you are an individual or organization who desires to be diversity competent, my two questions for you are:

- How much will it cost you to become diversity competent?

- What price are you willing to pay to become diversity competent as an individual and as an organization?

Let me clarify what I mean by how much and what price. My questions are not solely aimed at your financial commitments to becoming diversity competent. My questions are aimed at the cost involved by making deep mental, emotional, educational and spiritual commitments and sacrifices toward becoming diversity competent as an individual or organization. Within this context, I am more concerned about what internal commitments and sacrifices individuals are willing to make to ensure that organizations and communities as a whole are creating diversity-friendly, inclusive and welcoming environments for everyone to thrive and succeed.

**Diversity
Skill**

Before Kelly and Kyle can prepare to develop diversity competence and skill proficiency, they must prepare to complete pillar # 4, which is developing their personal and professional diversity skills. *Possessing diversity skills implies that individuals and organizations have the ability to apply their diversity knowledge appropriately and effectively during diversity encounters and interactions.* I've found that many individuals and organizations want to advance straight to developing their personal and professional diversity skills without legitimately exploring, understanding and embracing the other three pillars of diversity: diversity will, diversity desire and diversity knowledge. The philosophy and practice of diversity competence teaches that each of the four pillars are interdependent upon one another, meaning individuals and organizations need ALL four of the pillars to be in complete diversity rhythm.

I am often asked by workshop participants, "Does an individual or organization really need to embrace all four pillars of diversity competence before becoming diversity competent?" I gregariously reply, "If an individual or organization desires to communicate and interact appropriately and effectively with their diverse clients, colleagues, customers, employees and students in an authentic, sincere and transparent manner, then it is imperative to embrace all four pillars of diversity competence. The four pillars all depend and rely on one another during effective diversity encounters and interactions."

One popular diversity follow-up question is: What if an individual or organization is not willing to explore, understand and embrace the first two pillars (diversity will and diversity desire)? With a large smile on my face and after taking a deep breathe I responded by saying, "Yes, I know there are individuals and organizations in our society that intentionally refuse to allow themselves to engage in diversity-related concerns, issues and topics. Many of their reasons are private ones, which prevent them from fully adopting the philosophy and practice of diversity competence. Those who do not fully make the commitment typically like to skip over diversity pillars #1 (diversity will) and #2 (diversity desire) and move directly to the less emotional pillars #3 (diversity knowledge) and #4 (diversity skills) because they are perceived as more practical and pragmatic and, once again, less emotionally and mentally taxing. Those who decide to skip over diversity pillars #1 and #2 are described by diverse clients, colleagues, customers, employees and students as diversity fakes, phonies and imposters because they can detect their insincerity and lack of authenticity before, during and after the diversity encounter and interaction."

Diversity competence is all about respect, understanding and mutual cooperation. However, as demonstrated through the example with Kelly and Kyle, this kind of competence will not fall into your lap because there is real work involved in becoming diversity competent. By using the conscious forces of diversity will and diversity desire, you can acquire the diversity knowledge and the diversity skills necessary to interact seamlessly with diverse people whose diversity dimensions are *unlike* your own.

> "Remember, no one can make you feel
> inferior without your consent."
> **Eleanor Roosevelt**

■   ■   ■

Part 3

Barriers to Diversity Competence

Diversity BAPS

Have you ever wondered why there are so many class action lawsuits and discrimination claims filed every day? Or why certain ethnic and racial groups are pulled over more often for routine traffic stops? Or why African-Americans are watched more often while shopping in retail stores? Or why some persons with disabilities are not promoted into visible and key leadership positions? Or why women are labeled as "bitches" when they are only being as assertive as their male counterparts during workplace meetings? If you are still unsure why inequities, mistreatments and unfairness still happen so often in life, school and work, it is because of our Diversity BAPS.

What are Diversity BAPS? *Diversity BAPS are personal and professional barriers that interfere with fair judgment, equal treatment and effective communication when interacting with diverse people.* Diversity BAPS is an acronym, which stands for Biases, Assumptions, Prejudices and Stereotypes.

Diversity BAPS Explained

Biases: These are personal preferences and fixed opinions we hold of **diverse people** that prevent fair and equal treatment.

Assumptions: These involve the act of accepting information about **diverse people** as fact or true without proof.

Prejudices: These involve opinions formed beforehand about **diverse people** without sufficient evidence and information.

Stereotypes: Stereotyping includes exaggerated beliefs and distorted generalizations made about a group of **diverse people**. These beliefs and perceptions regarding a group of **diverse people** are most often negative. However, stereotypes can be both positive and negative, but both have limitations.

Oops...I Really Didn't Mean It: The Michael Richards Story

Michael Richards was an undeniably famous comedian. As the crazy Kramer on the hit TV show "Seinfeld," he enjoyed legions of fans from all walks of life. In November of 2006, he performed standup comedy at the Laugh Factory in West Hollywood.

Shortly after starting his show, he was playfully heckled by a group of African-American fans that had come to see the show. Richards, for whatever reason, appeared to be aggressive, snappy and on edge that night. He began screaming at the African-American hecklers saying, "Fifty years ago we'd have you upside down with a f***king fork up your ass." He continued to refer to the gentlemen as "niggers" and seemed unable to stop his tirade against the hecklers. Many of the audience members left after his tirade, apparently disgusted by what Richards was saying.

Later, on the Letterman Show, Richards stated, "For me to be at a comedy club and flip out and say this kind of crap, I'm deeply, deeply sorry." Later he said, "I'm not a racist. That's what's so insane about this." Many African-Americans were not impressed with Richards' apology.

This is yet another negative consequence of what can happen when you fail to overcome your Diversity BAPS (Biases, Assumptions, Prejudices and Stereotypes). While you may be able to hide them when you are not experiencing any stress, just a bit of stress or the wrong circumstances can have you verbally or non-verbally communicating your true DA (Diversity Attitude). Michael Richards seems to believe (and want us to believe) that he is not racist. Apparently, he did not have a deep understanding or personal connection regarding his Diversity BAPS. Instead, he shared them with the rest of the world under circumstances where his stress level tore down the interpersonal walls of his Diversity BAPS. Altogether, this was definitely a lose-lose situation.

How Dangerous and Destructive are Diversity BAPS?

Diversity BAPS create major barriers and problems in daily encounters and interactions. Diversity BAPS determine how an individual communicates, interacts and treats people in her or his personal and professional life. Submitting to one's Diversity BAPS is one of the leading causes of hate crimes, social injustices and workplace discrimination. It may be something relatively benign, such as how you address a person or look at someone, or something very serious, like whether or not you will hire or promote someone within your organization or admit someone who is different from you into your country club, fraternity or sorority.

Here is an example of how I was impacted by someone's Diversity BAPS:

Black Me and Rap Music

I, Jermaine M. Davis, am guilty of shopping while black and purchasing rap music. I began purchasing rap and R&B music in January of 1993 every Tuesday (the official weekday when new music is released and sold in retail stores) as a graduate student at the University of Wisconsin-Superior. I was researching the rhetorical communication in rap music and hip-hop culture and its effects on popular culture; purchasing rap music was significant to my research. There were times when I would spend hours analyzing, evaluating and gazing through hundreds of CDs before making a purchase. I desired quality research material to help me write a groundbreaking thesis, which I titled, "What is this Rap Shit? A Descriptive and Historical Analysis of Rap Music and Hip-Hop Culture."

After months of shopping for rap music at the same three retail stores in Superior, Wisconsin and Duluth, Minnesota (both predominantly white cities with very little diversity in 1993), I realized I was being watched aggressively. No one in the stores ever professionally introduced herself or himself to me, but they sure watched the rap section and me very closely. Initially I was appalled, but I would immediately forget about their unprofessional behavior and dismiss their diversity incompetence because I was more focused on acquiring music for my thesis research.

Sometimes I visited these three retail stores several times a week. The more I shopped, the more I thought my shopping and customer service experience would improve. Unfortunately, it never did! My emotions escalated from being an appalled customer to being an agitated, irritated, frustrated and on-edge when I entered the three stores. What was even more frustrating about my situation was the fact that I was your typical poor college student that spent my entire work-study paycheck on rap music to support my graduate research. I was financially supporting businesses that were not diversity-friendly, inclusive and welcoming to me as a customer of color. I would spend hundreds of dollars each month supporting the only three stores that sold hip-hop and rap music at that time in Superior, Wisconsin and Duluth, Minnesota.

How did I feel as a 21-year-old black kid from the inner city of Chicago buying rap music in Superior, Wisconsin and Duluth, Minnesota in 1993? I felt unwanted, unwelcome and uncomfortable as a shopper and as a customer of color. I made a huge assumption that my track record had communicated to the retailers that I was a legitimate weekly customer who was not a shoplifter because I made cash payments for every CD I ever purchased. I never bounced a check, had a declined credit card or ever used counterfeit money. I was "all-good" as the slang phrase goes; however, I was still guilty of shopping while being black. Unfortunately, I felt demonized, devalued, demeaned and disrespected as a customer of color. I felt this way because I knew as a person of color I was under suspicion because of the color of my skin. I knew I was singled-out and became the focus of the store's attention because of my race. I knew my skin color, tone and complexion made me a prime target.

Whatever the Diversity BAPS the store managers and sales people held of young black men motivated them to follow me around. Sometimes I would test my assumptions by changing locations throughout the store and–you guessed it–the store personnel would change their location as I changed locations. They would pretend as if they had work to do in every location I appeared as a shopper of color. Sometimes I would participate and play the profile game with the store personnel (often making silly faces at store cameras), but many times I did not play the profile game because it became too taxing and vexing for me mentally, emotionally and physically.

The managers and sales associates, who were all white, allowed their Diversity BAPS to interfere with me having a great customer service experience as I shopped in their retail stores. As I write this story I am thinking to myself, "How sick were you, Jermaine, to allow yourself to be victimized and dehumanized on a weekly basis for an entire year?" Growing up in Chicago, one of the most segregated cities in the United States, taught me one huge lesson on race, which is as a black man, it is important to know when you are being *celebrated* as a person of color and when you are being *tolerated* as a person of color. This lesson was key to my safety when I left the confines of Chicago's west side (a predominantly African-American area). This lesson taught me to persevere despite my diversity adversities and challenges; plus I had a one hundred page thesis to write and I refused to allow a few diversity incompetent managers and sales people to stand in the way of me achieving my dreams, goals and aspirations.

Unchecked and uncontrollable Diversity BAPS in similar cases have led to high profile discrimination cases costing schools and organizations millions and billions of dollars not to mention tarnished reputations, both professionally and socially. This is why individuals within schools and organizations need diversity training and coaching to help them become more aware of their Diversity BAPS to prevent unfair and unjust treatment and disrespectful communication from occurring with colleagues, customers, employees and students. People cannot change negative attitudes and behaviors that they are not cognizant of. Awareness and acknowledgement of one's Diversity BAPS is a prerequisite for becoming diversity competent. To assess your own diversity awareness, ask yourself the following questions: Are you aware of your Diversity BAPS? Have you acknowledged your Diversity BAPS?

Examples of Dangerous and
Destructive Diversity BAPS

The following examples are demonstrations of how Diversity BAPS can lead to discrimination in life, school and work. When individuals' Diversity BAPS are unchecked, uncontrolled and unmonitored, they will cause individuals and organizations to discriminate consciously and unconsciously. Diversity BAPS can determine who is hired or not hired, promoted or not promoted, whose loan is approved or not approved, who is rented to or not rented to, who is granted access or denied access, who is profiled or not profiled, who is granted leniency or dealt with strictly and who is allowed opportunities or stripped of opportunities.

Example #1:
I Just Need a Place to Rest My Head!

Can your race and ethnicity determine where you live and rest your head at night? Yes, race and ethnicity can determine your living arrangement and location. African-Americans and Latinos are often denied fair and equal access to apartments, homes, mortgage loans and insurance, according to The National Fair Housing Alliance (NFHA). African-Americans and Latinos are more likely than any other race to be discriminated against when seeking to purchase a home or rent an apartment. The National Fair Housing Alliance (NFHA) found that 32% of all housing discrimination was racially-driven and motivated. A similar study validated this statistic in an article published in *DiversityInc* entitled, "One Third of Blacks, and Latinos Face Racism in Housing." The article states:

> "…The Fair Housing Trends Report looked at 23,500 complaints lodged with NFHA members last year. It indicates race was the most commonly reported basis for housing discrimination in the United States (32% of all complaints). The housing discrimination took on various forms, some subtler than others. In some instances, real estate agents only showed homes to African-American or Latino home buyers in predominantly minority communities. Other reports included examples where

sellers were unwilling to negotiate the price of a home when offers were made by African-Americans or Latinos, but were willing to do so with white buyers. In some reports, sellers took their homes off the market in order to avoid a sale to a person of color. With apartment rentals, frequent reports of discrimination included denying that rental units were available; quoting higher rents or security deposits, and segregating African-Americans and Latinos in one part of a building or complex."

These statistics provide surprising proof of how Diversity BAPS can impact people of color and their opportunity to fair housing.

Example #2:
I'm Sorry I Don't Have a Voice of Choice!

Did you know that the sound of your voice may result in unfair treatment? Does the sound of a person's voice make them a more likely candidate for discrimination? Does having an accent, speaking a different dialect or sounding "too ethnic" work against certain individuals in America? Absolutely, absolutely, absolutely! Individuals and organizations that discriminate against individuals because of their accent, dialect or sounding "too ethnic" are practicing the discriminatory act of linguistic profiling.

Professor John Baugh is highly respected for his groundbreaking study and research on the topic of linguistic profiling. Baugh, a professor of education and linguistics at Stanford University, was compelled and motivated to research this aspect of language discrimination when he first moved to Palo Alto, CA. When Professor Baugh would call a property using his educated and professional voice (or "white" sounding voice), he would be told that the property was available. He found that property managers would change their mind when they

> "People should not feel they need to mask their linguistic background. You should be free to speak in whatever way is comfortable for you and not experience discrimination because of it."
> **Professor John Baugh**

saw him in person. Professor and researcher John Baugh is African-American.

So what was Professor Baugh's study all about? According to the *RACE* Exhibit, A Project of the American Anthropological Association, "In the 1990s, he conducted a series of tests in which people who spoke with what he termed "African-American Venacular English," "Chicano English" and "Standard American English" accents phoned to answer newspaper ads for jobs and apartments. Often the African-American Venacular English and Chicano English callers who left messages were not called back or were told that the job or apartment was no longer available even when the standard American English speaker was told that it was still available."

In addition, Patrice D. Johnson wrote an article entitled, "Linguistic Profiling," that captures Baugh's experience. She writes, "Call it TWB–Talking While Black. A person has a telephone conversation with someone he has never seen before and draws a conclusion about the race of that person solely on the way the person sounds."

Regarding language and discrimination, Professor Baugh continues to say, "We can usually tell if a person is a man, a woman, young or old, a southerner or a Latino in the space of a five-minute telephone conversation. But linguistic profiling is somebody acting upon that racial or demographic imprint in a criminal way by denying (the victims) access to a business transaction that should not be in any way biased, based on a person's racial background."

His own personal experience with linguistic profiling occurred a few years ago when he was looking for a place to live in California. He would call up in response to an ad in the newspaper, but when he would show up, he would learn that the apartment was unavailable. He believes that it is because over the phone, when he uses his "professional voice," he sounds "white." When he appeared in person, he was handed all sorts of excuses for why he could not rent—none being, of course, the obvious fact that he was black.

So Baugh went about trying to prove what he had suspected. Having grown up in the inner city of Philadelphia and Los Angeles, Baugh was exposed to a variety of ethnic dialects and considers himself "linguistically dexterous." He began telephoning renters and would say, "Hello, I'm calling about the apartment you have advertised in the paper." He would make some calls using his professional voice. Other times he would modify his voice, repeating the same sentence with the same grammar, but with an intonation that was unmistakably black. He made more than one hundred calls and found that his "black" voice got half as many calls back as his "white" voice. It did not matter that when Baugh used his black voice, he was speaking perfect, standard English.

In commenting on the vocal racial inequity, Baugh says, "Apparently, if a speaker on the telephone sounds African-American, he is subject to the same kind of racial discrimination as he might be in a face-to-face encounter."

Example #3: Working While GLBT (Gay, Lesbian, Bisexual and Transgender)

Does being a heterosexual in the workplace interfere with an individual's upward mobility and organizational success? Absolutely not! Can being a member of the GLBT (Gay, Lesbian, Bisexual and Transgender) community in the workplace interfere with an individual's upward mobility and organizational success? Absolutely yes!

To be quite frank, many organizations and schools still avoid the topic of how to best welcome, include and support gay colleagues and employees. Yes, there have been improvements in some organizations, but many GLBT employees still have to worry and wonder about their personal, professional and physical safety and well-being in the workplace. Being open about one's sexual orientation in the workplace can have many severe and negative consequences for GLBT colleagues and employees. Many GLBT colleagues and employees remain quiet or closeted about their sexual orientation in the workplace due to workplace hostility and intolerance, to keep their jobs, to advance their careers and to prevent GLBT harassment. However, the thought-provoking question still remains, is gay bashing and discrimination the last permissible bias and prejudice in America?

When considering GLBT discrimination, it is important that individuals and organizations understand that the philosophy and practice of diversity competence does not force individuals to change their beliefs, but it teaches individuals and organizations to examine and understand how beliefs impact and influence personal and professional behaviors. When I conduct diversity workshops at schools and organizations, my main goal is to get colleagues, employees and students thinking about their behaviors towards diverse people. There is a direct correlation between beliefs, behaviors and the act of discrimination. Denying a person access and opportunity because of their sexual orientation in the workplace is discrimination, which is against the law.

Individuals who are opposed to members of the GLBT community may never change their beliefs, but they can self-edit, self-monitor and change any unacceptable behaviors expressed toward those in the GLBT community. The formidable task of persuading someone to change her or his core beliefs on an ingrained value can be almost impossible *if* not impossible. Organizations cannot regulate employees' *beliefs*, but they can regulate employees' *behaviors*. Organizations can clearly spell out acceptable and unacceptable behaviors for their employees in their company literature. It is important for employees and students to comprehend that they can *believe* whatever they want in the workplace or at school, but they cannot, and I repeat they cannot *behave* any way they want in the workplace or at school without breaking and violating laws and violating civil and human rights.

What happens when a human resource professional's Diversity BAPS targeted at GLBT employees goes unchecked, unmonitored and unregulated? Employment discrimination occurs when a GLBT employee's rights, access and opportunity to fair employment is denied because of their sexual orientation. This does not happen in real life, *does* it? According to an article in *DiversityInc* written by Kipp Cheng entitled, "Creating 'Safe Spaces' for GLBT Employees in the Workplace," employment discrimination does happen in the workplace. Cheng writes:

> *"The fear for GLBT workers was confirmed in a NGLTF (National Gay and Lesbian Task Force) survey of 191 employers that revealed biases against workers based on their sexual orientation: When asked how the revelation of a gay, lesbian or bisexual employee's sexual orientation would affect an employer's opinion of the worker, 18 percent of employers said they would fire, 27 percent would refuse to hire and 26 percent would refuse to promote a person perceived to be gay, lesbian or bisexual."*

I shared this survey with an audience once and, during my presentation, a gentleman in the very last row of the 600-seat auditorium raised his hand and said, "I have more of a comment than a question and that is, no matter what you say, you will not and cannot change my beliefs and views on homosexuality." I responded by saying, "Thank you for sharing your comments, but I was not invited here to change people's beliefs and values. I was invited here to talk about my book *Be Diversity Competent,* and part of being diversity competent is being aware of how your beliefs can impact and influence your behaviors. I know I cannot change your beliefs and values, sir, but I want everyone in the audience to know that their behaviors can lead to discrimination, a disengaged workforce and a costly legal bill for your organization."

Discovering Your Diversity BAPS

Have you ever thought about what Diversity BAPS (Biases, Assumptions, Prejudices and Stereotypes) you may hold of diverse people who are different from you? If so, and you want to move from diversity incompetence to diversity competence, then answer and respond to the group categories in the following exercise.

1st Thoughts Exercise

Using a one-word adjective or descriptor whether positive or negative, write down the 1st thought that comes to your mind when you think of, communicate and interact with individuals from the following categories:

Traditionalists (Born between 1922-1945) _____

Baby Boomers (Born between 1946-1964)_____

Generation Xers (Born between 1965-1980) _____

Millennials (Born between 1981-2000) _____

Christians _____

Muslims _____

Atheists _____

Buddhists _____

Immigrants and Refugees _____

Men _____

Women _____

Democrats _____

Republicans_____

Interracial Couples _____

Single Mothers with Multiple Children _____

GLBT (Gays, Lesbians, Bisexuals and Transgender) _____

Persons with Disabilities_____

Persons living with HIV/AIDS _____

Individuals from Urban Communities _____

Individuals from Suburban Communities_____

Individuals from Farming and Rural Communities _____

Individuals with Tattoos and Body Piercings_____

Individuals with Different Accents/Dialects _____

Individuals You Perceive to be Obese and Overweight _____

Individuals Who are Upper Class (Socio-Economics)_____

Individuals Who are Middle Class (Socio-Economics) _____

Individuals Who are Lower Class (Socio-Economics)_____

African-Americans _____

Asian Americans_____

Jewish Americans _____

Latinos and Latinas_____

Middle Easterners _____

Native Americans _____

White Americans _____

Now examine your list of positive and negative one-word adjectives and descriptors and ask yourself, "Why do I feel the way I do or think the way I do regarding certain communities of diverse people? The first emotions you feel, and the 1st thoughts you think of when communicating and interacting with any of the above mentioned groups reflects the Diversity BAPS you have stored consciously and unconsciously regarding the diverse people you are interacting with. The Diversity BAPS you hold of diverse people can be extremely dangerous because Diversity BAPS don't take into account the individual you are communicating and interacting with. The person is treated as a group category rather than an individual. My goal as author of this book is to help you and organizations become aware of their Diversity BAPS, so you can develop a plan to overcome them and communicate more competently and effectively with diverse people.

Why We Use the 1st Thoughts Exercise

The objective of this exercise is to help you become more acquainted with and cognizant of your Diversity BAPS to prevent personal, professional and social injustices from occurring when you are communicating and interacting with diverse people. Diversity BAPS create enormous interpersonal conflicts in life, school and work. Becoming aware of and acknowledging one's Diversity BAPS is key toward eliminating them. The 1st Thoughts Exercise was designed to help you and organizations move from diversity ignorance to diversity awareness with the ultimate goal of helping individuals and organizations become diversity competent.

If learning and understanding about one's Diversity BAPS does not seem to be an important issue to you in today's communities, schools and organizations, try the following exercise. As you read it, pay close attention to the feelings and thoughts that are triggered inside you.

⟶ Try this exercise!

Scenario:

You are responsible for hiring employees for a small staffing agency. Recently, you received job requisitions on your desk to fill two open positions. Based on your time and interview availability, you only have openings to interview four of the ten candidates who have applied for the position.

You have reviewed all the potential candidates' resumes and applications and have determined that all of the candidates meet your personal criteria and the professional qualifications needed for the open positions.

Let us now take a look at the names and ages of the applicants.

Applicants:

(1)   James Johnson: Age 28
(2)   Marge Jenkins: Age 61
(3)   Sheniqua Brown: Age 23
(4)   Mohammed Jabaar: Age 30
(5)   Jesus Mendoza: Age 45
(6)   William Big Horn: Age 50
(7)   Lilly White: Age 29 (Your secretary knows her; she is openly gay).
(8)   Pao Lue Vang: Age 40
(9)   Michael Friedman: Age 31
(10) Daniel Hunter: Age 35

Questions:

Who will you choose to interview?

Who do you think would be the best candidate for this position (which will involve customer service?

Do not worry! There is no right or wrong answer to this exercise. The purpose of this exercise is to help you understand how intricately diversity is woven into our unconscious mind and society and how our Diversity BAPS (Biases, Assumptions, Prejudices and Stereotypes) affect our decision-making. Diversity characteristics can be as simple as name, age, gender or sexual orientation and can negatively color your perceptions of diverse people and influence your ability to make fair and equitable decisions.

Can Diversity BAPS interfere with a person's job search? You better believe it! Can a hiring manger's Diversity BAPS prevent her or him from granting a job interview or from returning a phone call to an interested job applicant because they have an ethnic sounding name? Absolutely! According to a study conducted by professors at the University of Chicago's Graduate School of Business and the Massachusetts Institute of Technology, it helps to have a white-sounding name when seeking employment. The white-sounding names in the study included: Anne, Brett, Emily, Greg, Jill and Neil. The black-sounding names included: Aisha, Ebony, Kareem, Rasheed, Tamika and Tyrone. The Associated Press wrote of the study:

> *"Resumes with white-sounding first names elicited 50 percent more responses than ones with black-sounding names ..." The professors sent about 5,000 resumes in response to want ads in the Boston Globe and Chicago Tribune. They found that the 'white' applicants they created received one response—a call, letter or e-mail for every 10 resumes mailed, while 'black' applicants with equal credentials received one response for every 15 resumes sent."*

University of Chicago Associate Professor of Economics Marianne Bertrand said, "The results can solely be attributed to name manipulation. Our results so far suggest that there is a substantial amount of discrimination [Diversity BAPS] in the job recruiting process."

The reality that diversity exists within our society is a fact you cannot change. What you *can* change, however, is how you choose to handle the diversity you will inevitably encounter and experience. This is important since diversity itself is not the problem; rather, it is the diversity *attitude* that individuals and organizations hold that determines if they will experience greater diversity conflict and tension in life, school and work. A negative diversity attitude is typically followed by intolerant actions. Shakespeare sums this notion up well with his quote, "There is nothing good or bad, but thinking so makes all the difference." So, what are your true diversity attitudes and perceptions as an individual and organization?

The Power of Diversity BAPS: The Mel Gibson Incident

July 26, 2006, was not a good day for Mel Gibson. Mr. Gibson was out past midnight speeding along the Pacific Coast Highway in his 2006 Lexus LS 430. In fact, he was speeding along at 87 miles per hour in a 45 mile per hour zone. When Mr. Gibson was pulled over, he was found to be carrying an open bottle of alcohol in his vehicle, and he had a blood alcohol level of 0.12%.

Mel Gibson initially cooperated with the arresting officer until he was arrested. It was at the point of arrest that he unleashed his Diversity BAPS (Biases, Assumptions, Prejudices and Stereotypes) and anger toward the officer. "Are you a Jew?" Mr. Gibson asked the officer. He continued to make remarks to the officer as well as other officers at the scene. The police report alleges that Mr. Gibson stated, "F***ing Jews...the Jews are responsible for all the wars in the world."

While he made a public apology the next day, there was an outcry within the Jewish community regarding Mr. Gibson's anti-Semitic remarks. In response, Gibson made a lengthy apology about a week after the incident. In spite of his apologies, Mr. Gibson was removed from an upcoming mini-series project on the Holocaust.

It is fair to say that Mel Gibson did not get to where he got in Hollywood by making anti-Semitic remarks on a regular basis when he was sober. It was only after losing a fair bit of inhibition that his Diversity BAPS became obvious. Unfortunately, for Mr. Gibson, the whole world found out about his Diversity BAPS.

Under tense emotional stress and under the influence of alcohol, his true Diversity BAPS caught up with him and cost him a great deal. Awareness and acknowledgement is critical to overcoming one's Diversity BAPS. While they may not come out in your speech, they definitely show up in your body language while communicating and interacting with diverse people. Stop your Diversity BAPS before you become front-page news!

Assessing Your Diversity BAPS

I often meet well-intentioned and good-hearted people who want to make the world a better and more inviting place for ALL people. These individuals are sometimes over-zealous, meaning they want to eradicate the injustices of the world so badly that they forget there are critical steps to follow in any transformational movement. The most overlooked step I hear and see is that some diversity proponents are so quick to recognize and point out other people's Diversity BAPS that they fail to discover, recognize and identify their own Diversity BAPS.

The discovery, recognition and acknowledgement of one's own Diversity BAPS is the number one prerequisite to preventing personal, professional and social injustices and inequities. I often tell audiences that if you are going to *truly* do the work of diversity and social justice, you must be sincere and truthfully ask yourself, "What are the biases, assumptions, prejudices and stereotypes I hold of diverse people?" I realize answering this question honestly and truthfully may make you feel ashamed, embarrassed and/or guilty; however, if you are going to do diversity work with conviction, it is imperative to be honest and truthful with yourself.

Let us now take a step closer to achieving our goal of becoming a diversity competent individual and explore an exercise that can assist you in uncovering your Diversity BAPS.

⟶ Try this exercise!

Study the statements in the following exercise, and answer them honestly to further identify your Diversity BAPS.

Answer each question honestly:	True	False	Don't Know
My race and culture are better than others.			
Asians are smart in math and science.			
Blacks do not speak English correctly.			
Women are too emotional to lead effectively.			
I do not like people who speak with strong foreign accents.			
Elderly people should be in a home where they can be cared for.			
Baby Boomers have lots of money.			
Teenagers get into trouble more often than not.			
Democrats despise corporate organizations and big business.			
Republicans despise social service programs.			
Unwed mothers are poor and not very intelligent.			
We have AIDS because of gays.			
Black people are great dancers and athletes.			
Native Americans are drunks.			
People from the Middle East hate Americans.			
Overweight people are lazier than slender people.			
Persons with disabilities are just loafing on Social Security.			
Immigrants are stealing our jobs.			
Black people are loud.			
Religious people are narrow-minded.			
Non-Christian people do not understand faith very well.			
People from New York are usually rude and abrasive.			
Canadians sound funny when they talk.			
Republicans are homophobic.			
Democrats are extremely liberal politicians.			
Middle Eastern people cannot be trusted.			
People in wheelchairs make me uncomfortable.			
Southerners are rednecks.			
People who like "monster trucks" are rednecks.			

Recovering alcoholics are not trustworthy.			
Educated people are egotistical snobs.			
Women are not as smart or as capable as men.			
Men spend most of their time thinking about sex.			
It is not worth hiring someone who is considered elderly.			
Blacks are responsible for most of the crime in this country.			
I do not feel comfortable around gay people.			
Mixed race people are generally from a broken home.			
People of color are getting jobs that whites should have.			
If you live in America, you should learn the language.			
Gays are okay, but they should not be able to adopt children.			
Mexicans have so many babies; they will soon be the majority.			

Though these statements represent only a sampling of Diversity BAPS that individuals may hold, they provide a great start in helping you identify your Diversity BAPS and to assist you on your diversity journey and quest toward becoming diversity competent. Review your responses carefully to get an honest and truthful evaluation of your Diversity BAPS.

In an effort to take you one step further in assessing your Diversity BAPS, please complete the following exercise describing yourself.

⟶ Try this exercise!

Who am I?

Please list your age, race, ethnicity, sexual orientation, gender and whether you are a person with a disability or not.

I am a _____

_____

_____

_____

Now name the group or category of individuals that you have diversity discomfort with.

Describe the feelings you feel. _____

_____

_____

List those things you found to be true about yourself in this exercise.

_____

_____

Your completed statement may read something like this: "I am a 32-year-old heterosexual Korean male with a physical disability (multiple sclerosis) that feels uncomfortable around people who are gay and people who are well-educated and are snobs, etc."

Phew! As hard as that may have been, you need to understand that you cannot make progress without knowing where you stand *currently*. Do not worry if you discover that you have more Diversity BAPS than you thought; *becoming aware of and acknowledging* your Diversity BAPS matters the most at this point.

Everything that Glitters Ain't Gold: The Susan Smith Story

Susan Smith was a young woman madly in love. Separated from her husband in 1994, she fell in love with a man who wanted to be with her, but he did not want anything to do with her three-year-old and one-year-old sons. So Susan Smith deviously concocted a plot to get her two sons out of her life. On October 25, 1994, she drove her car with her two boys strapped in the back seat into a lake in South Carolina.

She played the role of a mentally anguished and emotionally distraught mother, stating that an African-American man, who then drove off with the children, had hijacked her car. It was only after several days of poor leads and inconsistencies in her story that she finally confessed and led police to the bodies of her two sons.

Why did Susan Smith select that particular ethnic group? Why did she think that her story was more believable when she claimed that the perpetrator was an African-American man? The fact remains that for several days, the story was quite believable.

In today's society, there remain certain dimensions of diversity that reinforce stereotypes we hold of specific groups. African-Americans, to some, are more believable as criminals because society has stereotyped them to be that way. If Susan Smith had said the perpetrator was a Caucasian man, would Americans have seen her story any differently? What if she said that the perpetrator was an Asian or a Latino man? Stereotypes, in spite of our attempts at accepting and embracing diversity, do still exist in our greater society. Are we more apt to believe an untrue story of an African-American hijacker than we are to believe that a woman could murder her own children out of love for another man. What role did Diversity BAPS play in this story?

The **FIRE** Barrier to Diversity Competence

Now that you have discovered and recognized a few of your Diversity BAPS, let us look at the various barriers preventing the achievement of true diversity competence in life, school and work. To explain this, I use the acronym "**FIRE.**" **FIRE** is what prevents diversity competence from occurring among individuals and organizations.

> **The FIRE Barrier to Diversity Competence**
> Fear
> Ignorance
> Resentment
> Ego

In life, real fires are dangerous, destructive and devastating to all their victims. The aftermath of a fire has the potential to negatively impact the person or property it encounters forever. Similarly, the **FIRE** Barrier to Diversity Competence is responsible for preventing millions of people from being diversity competent, both personally and professionally.

The **FIRE** Barrier to Diversity Competence was designed to help individuals and organizations understand the reality of why people cannot get along in life, school and work. The issues explained in the **FIRE** Barrier to Diversity Competence are typically hush-hush topics when addressed in many public arenas, but nonetheless, I have addressed them in an appropriate and professional manner to help individuals and organizations move from diversity chaos and conflict to diversity communication and cooperation.

FIRE - The Diversity Barrier of Fear

Fear and Fear of the Unknown

The first barrier to diversity competence in the **FIRE** acronym is *fear*. Fear, fear, fear—we hear and read about this emotion all the time, but many writers do not define the word. Fear is an anxiety-based emotion either real or perceived aroused by danger, harm or pain. ***Diversity fear is when individuals and organizations experience uneasiness when communicating and interacting with diverse people that they are not used to.*** If individuals and organizations are not used to your diversity, then your diversity is unknown to them, which gives birth to the phrase "fear of the unknown."

In general, fear of the unknown arises because most people prefer predictability and not surprises. Learning about new cultures and new dimensions of diversity different from what we are familiar with can cause great diversity anxiety, discomfort and uneasiness for some people. Additionally, much of what is least understood (for whatever reason) is feared either openly or secretly. I love the quote, "People fear what they do not understand," because it describes this idea very well.

I first wrote about the effects of how fear of the unknown could be personally debilitating in my book *Get Up Off Your Butt & Do It NOW!: Staying Motivated*

Even When You Don't Feel Like It. In this book, I explained how fear of the unknown sabotages millions of people's dreams, goals and aspirations because individuals willingly submit to familiarity. Fear of the unknown prevents millions of individuals and organizations from being diversity-friendly, inclusive and welcoming each and every day.

Consider how I explained the debilitating emotion of fear in my first book, and as you read the text, imagine how fear of the unknown sabotages diversity efforts regularly. *The fear of the unknown is the fear of entering and embarking upon uncharted, unfamiliar and unknown territory.* This fear prevents people from taking risks, trying new things and exploring new avenues in life. On the other hand, the known are things we have previous knowledge of—things that provide predictability and comfort, things we have personal experience with and things that are familiar to our daily experiences. People's minds are especially secure with the known because the known is certain, comfortable, common, familiar and predictable, and individuals feel more confident and relaxed when they are functioning within known boundaries.

I believe the core reason people have a fear of the unknown is because they cannot control and predict the outcome of certain situations. This lack of control breeds feelings of anxiety, uncertainty, stress and perceived helplessness. I believe this is the key factor that gives the fear of the unknown its power and strength. People feel extremely uneasy and uncomfortable when they do not know what to expect in a given situation—when they cannot see how something is going to turn out from start to finish.

For example, you are working with someone for the first time whose cultural background is unfamiliar to you. Without taking time to gain an understanding about her or his culture, you may experience diversity awkwardness and discomfort lasting until a comfort level with the diverse person is established. Diversity tension can be reduced through education, personal encounters and personal experiences. When I mention education, I mean learning more about the person and their diversity through formal and informal education. When I mention experience, I mean deliberately engaging in interpersonal encounters with diverse people to reduce your diversity anxiety, fear and uncertainty.

Here is an example of diversity fear and how this fear can impact how you interact with diverse individuals in life, school and work.

The Praying Doctor

A diversity situation fueled by fear occurred a few years ago in a rural Midwest town with a population of nearly all white Christian Americans. The local hospital invited a specialist in otolaryngology to provide ear, nose and throat medical services to patients on a weekly basis. This new doctor was from the Middle East. While the staff found him to be an excellent and skilled physician, they quickly found themselves in a diversity dilemma. The doctor requested time off during his workday to pray for religious and spiritual reasons, which caused diversity discomfort for the staff.

Initially, the nurses working with him were fearful because he was a doctor and a respected professional and they felt they could not approach him and ask him firsthand questions about his faith and prayer time. This became a workplace problem because there was a lack of communication and understanding among the colleagues and employees. A combination of fear, diversity discomfort and a lack of communication left the staff members unable to schedule the physician's patient appointments because they didn't know when his prayer times were occurring.

Fortunately, the CEO of the hospital did not share the same diversity discomfort and fear as everyone else. She asked the physician what his religious needs were and arrangements were made for the doctor to have solitary use of the doctor's lounge at set times of the day for prayer. Eventually, everyone understood the doctor's routine, resulting in reducing the earlier diversity fear and discomfort surrounding this aspect of his unique diversity.

"Fear is a disease that eats away at logic and makes man inhuman."
Marian Anderson

Fear and Homophobia

So what is homophobia? *Homophobia is the irrational fear or hatred of gays and lesbians.* The focus of the fear is targeted at the person's sexual orientation, which means the homophobic individual does not see the person as a human being (female or male) but rather as a sexual being. In other cases, the fear of a person's sexual orientation is so intense that it causes the fear-based heterosexual person to believe that the gay person will attempt to "turn" them into being gay as well (This is as if being gay is contagious and can "rub off" onto heterosexuals). This is a classic case of what I call radical and utter diversity ignorance.

Supposedly the gay person, through mere communication, manipulation and magic possesses the power to convert heterosexuals into being gay. Now explain the rationale in this argument. Would that imply that members of the gay community should be 'heterophobic' because if they work with, go to school with and live in close proximity to heterosexuals, there may be a chance *they* are plotting and scheming on how to best "turn" gays into "heterosexuals?" Homophobic individuals and organizations cannot and, *I repeat*, cannot become diversity competent if they are full of diversity fear and discomfort when communicating and interacting with members of the GLBT community.

What About the Religious Folk?

The question remains, can extremely religious folks become diversity competent in the area of sexual orientation if their theology teaches them that members of the GLBT community are hell-bound? I believe they can! Let me first start by acknowledging that I truly believe the quote, "You cannot change people." I cannot change people, nor can you change people. So what motivates people to change? People are compelled to change when *they* decide to change. People change because of their *own* motivation and values not because of *your* motivation and values. After being on the road for over a decade and conducting many diversity workshops and seminars, I have come face-to-face with hundreds of people who have declared to me, "Jermaine I don't care what you say or what any other diversity trainer says, you will not change my religious and personal beliefs about gays. My religion and my personal beliefs tell me that being gay is wrong and sinful."

When I work with individuals who possess a negative
or intolerant attitude towards members of the GLBT
community, I remind them of the laws, policies, rules,
regulations and civil and human rights that MUST be
adhered to. No, we cannot change the *belief system* of
these GLBT intolerant people, but we can change their
behavioral practices toward gays (in the workplace and

> "No one loves
> the man whom
> he fears."
> **Aristotle**

school setting). Will you still experience resistance from some people? Absolutely!
However, my goal is to create safe neighborhoods, houses of faith and worship,
schools and workplaces for those in the GLBT community.

Fear and Xenophobia

Another common diversity-related fear is xenophobia. ***Xenophobia is the fear of
specific or all types of foreigners (immigrants and refugees)***. Xenophobia may
manifest as a fear of the unknown or in more profound ways as evidenced in the
following statement, "I'm afraid that foreigners (immigrants and refugees) will take
over and take all the good jobs away from us Americans." Xenophobia becomes a
diversity-related barrier that interferes with good communication and workplace
equality. Individuals and organizations must address xenophobia promptly and
appropriately through understanding the culture of the feared group. Remember,
individuals and organizations fear what they do not understand and whatever they
perceive as threatening to them they avoid, resist and run away from.

In one of my favorite diversity-related books, *Racism Explained to My Daughter*,
author Tahar Ben Jelloun explains xenophobia in this way:

> *"The word 'foreigner' comes from the word 'foreign,' which
> means 'from the outside.' It means someone who's not part of the
> family, who doesn't belong to the clan or the tribe. A foreigner is
> someone who comes from another country—it can be nearby or
> far away, or sometimes just from another city or village. This is
> where we get the word 'xenophobia,' which means being hostile
> to foreigners, to anyone who comes from a foreign county."*

Why does diversity conflict and tension arise as new immigrants pursue their piece of the American Dream and American Pie as previous immigrants coming through Ellis Island did? There are some natural-born U.S. citizens who possess a Diversity Attitude (DA) of apathy, where they do not care about the advancement and personal and professional success of diverse people who are not like them. Their DA of apathy is intertwined with xenophobic beliefs.

In the magazine *Immigration in Minnesota,* diversity conflict and tension regarding xenophobia is explained the following way, "Some ...may feel resentment or competition towards relative newcomers who appear to be surpassing them economically. Others may fear that already scarce resources will be spread even more thinly as services such as job training and English language instruction are provided to new immigrants. And some people are simply intolerant of cultural differences."

So are the new immigrants depleting resources that natural-born citizens need? Well, the same article respectfully addresses this question by stating:

> *"It's true there are significant short-term costs associated with immigration. With the resettlement of refugees in particular, education, job training, health care, and other support systems must adapt to meet new and complex needs. The long-term economic benefits, however, more than offset those costs. Immigrants contribute to the economy in multiple ways: by paying taxes, filling job vacancies, engaging in entrepreneurial activities and neighborhood revitalization, and also through the consumption of goods and services. Since the majority of immigrants arrive at a young working age, they contribute to the economy for decades, often while remaining ineligible to receive some social service benefits."*

Why Do Immigrants Come to the U.S.?

People come to the United States of America because the U.S. has been historically coined, "The Land of Opportunity" and from a survival of the fittest perspective, opportunity of a better life naturally drives immigration and relocation. It seems to be in the mental, emotional and physical DNA of every human being to seek greater opportunities whenever possible. I left the west side of Chicago and relocated to Wisconsin and finally Minnesota to pursue better opportunities in life, school and work.

The new or most recent immigrants of America come for the same reasons as previous immigrants—for the opportunity to live a better life for themselves and their families. The Minneapolis Foundation writes of new immigrants, "...they experience the same difficulties of adjusting to life in a new country—language barriers, culture shock, a sense of loss, and isolation." Millions of Americans enjoy America today because our grandparents and great-grandparents of yesterday were allowed to pass through the doors of Ellis Island to begin a brand new life. Remember...the ultimate goal of immigrants is to advance personally and professionally in life, school and work.

How Soon We Forget: Ellis Island

Are immigrants taking American jobs and depleting American resources? Immigrant proponents and opponents go head to head over these controversial issues daily. Entire social and political campaigns are designed around the issue of immigration. Many want immigrants to leave, many want immigrants to stay and many do not have an opinion at all.

Who do you think of when you think of an immigrant? Are they poor? Are they uneducated? Are they criminals? Are they a bit strange in their philosophies? Do they speak broken English? Do you feel that taxpayer money is keeping immigrants from Mexico, Cuba, Thailand, Vietnam, Somalia or Africa in your neighborhoods?

How many people think of Ellis Island, the entrance point, for all the people who migrated from Norway, Scandinavia, Ireland, Germany or Austria to start new lives in the United States of America? These were our ancestors (many were our parents and/or grandparents) who came with their own sets of philosophies and traditions. Many did not speak the language and almost all were poor when they passed through Ellis Island as a brand new immigrant to America. They took American jobs—often those jobs that nobody else wanted—and they brought their cultural practices, traditional holidays and traditional dress. Unless you are Native American, there is a great chance that you descended from immigrants of other countries.

Is there a difference between the immigrants who went through Ellis Island and passed by the great Statue of Liberty and those who have crossed over the border from Mexico or took flight here from Somalia? Does the phrase, "Give me your tired, your poor..." no longer apply in this great country affectionately called The United States of America?

If we applied the same intensity of emotion we feel around Ellis Island to the immigration issues we are dealing with today, it is quite possible that some of our apathy, resentment and hatred would melt away and we would see immigration in a different light. Only through understanding the motivations and issues of our past ancestors can we really see through the eyes of those who desire to reside in the United States today. How soon do we forget?

Defining Relevant Immigration Language

How much do you really know about immigration? In an effort to help you on your diversity journey of understanding immigration, I have outlined nine terms I believe diversity competent individuals and organizations should know to eliminate the fear of xenophobia.

The definitions were taken from and explained clearly in a magazine article published by The Minneapolis Foundation entitled, "Immigration in Minnesota: Discovering Common Ground." Let us help eradicate immigration ignorance by examining and studying the following glossary of immigration terms.

Glossary of Immigration Terms

Immigration Term	Definition
Refugee	A person who is unable or unwilling to live in her or his native country because of persecution or a well-founded fear of persecution on the account of race, religion, nationality, membership in a particular social group or political opinion. Like many countries, the U.S. has made a commitment to allowing refugees to settle here.
Immigrant	A person who moves to a country where she or he intends to settle permanently. Legal immigrants have the permission of the U.S. government to live in America. Undocumented or illegal immigrants, do not.
Guest or Temporary Worker	A person who has temporary permission to work in the U.S.
Visa	A legal permit to enter the U.S. There are many different types of visas, granted according to the purpose, such as travel, work or study.
Foreign-Born Person	A U.S. resident who was not a citizen at birth.
Undocumented Worker	A person living and working in the U.S. without legal permission to do so.
Green Card	A colloquial term for the permit that enables someone who is not a citizen to live and work in the U.S.

Reunification	The process by which citizens and legal immigrants, including refugees, are allowed to sponsor close relatives, enabling them to come live in the U.S. Every year, approximately two-thirds of this country's legal immigrants join family members already living here.
Naturalization	The process by which an immigrant becomes a U.S. citizen. With a few exceptions (such as the right to run for president), naturalized citizens have all the rights, privileges, and responsibilities as native-born citizens.

Watch Your Hate Odometer!

Have you ever had a negative diversity encounter? What about a conflict or debate over the steaming controversial issue of same-sex marriage? Have you ever been involved in a racial conflict? How about an immigration conflict? Did your diversity-related conflicts evoke anger, aggression and frustration inside of you? If you have ever had a bad diversity experience, it is important to watch your hate odometer. An odometer is a device used to measure and record the speed of a moving vehicle. Likewise, *a hate odometer is an internal assessment and measurement of one's own thoughts and emotions after experiencing diversity conflict and tension.*

The first emotion following a bad diversity conflict or experience is anger, which is a neutral feeling—an emotion that can be either good or bad. But, without careful attention, anger can turn into resentment. And unchecked resentment develops into bitterness, resulting in hard feelings toward the diversity you are struggling with or experiencing diversity conflict with. This 'settling-in' of feelings can escalate into hate, and hate can be translated into crimes thus creating hate crimes.

Unfortunately, when these feelings continue to escalate, going unchecked and unmonitored, hate crimes and bias crimes occur. What exactly are hate and bias crimes? According to the Federal Hate Crimes Statistics Act of 1990, "*hate and*

bias crimes are crimes motivated by hatred against a victim based on [her or his] race, religion, sexual orientation, ethnicity or national origin." The Minnesota Attorney General's Office says this of hate crimes, "Hate crimes are based on fear, misunderstanding or dislike of a certain group of people." Some of the types of hate and bias crimes that are committed include:

- Murders
- Arsons
- Vandalism
- Physical Assault

Hate and bias crimes are often heinous. Spurred by deep-seated anger and intense hostility and hatred, hate crimes are most often committed with objects such as bats, bottles, bricks, knives and butts of guns. Some examples of hate and bias-motivated crimes include:

- Vandalism of a church, synagogue, mosque, temple or cemetery.
- An attack on an individual because of her or his accent.
- Assaulting a person believed to be a member of the GLBT community.
- Cross burning on a lawn.

Hate and bias-motivated crimes are motivated and directed towards a particular group of people. The top five categories targeted for hate and bias crimes are:

(1) Race
(2) Religion
(3) Sexual Orientation
(4) Ethnicity/National Origin
(5) Disabilities

Remember, hate and bias-motivated crimes are not ordinary types of crimes. Hate and bias-motivated crimes are motivated by hatred against an individual based upon her or his national origin, ethnicity, disability, race, religion and sexual orientation. These crimes result when people, fueled by the internal hate they feel, begin to inflict pain on other people due to their strong displeasure toward them. The following are two examples of hate and bias-motivated crimes resulting from unchecked and unmonitored hate odometers.

A Disturbing Death in Jasper, Texas

It was 1998 in Jasper Texas, and James Byrd, Jr. walked the long road home after enjoying a get-together with family and friends. He was intoxicated. He was tipsy, but a responsible drinker. He was walking—not driving—under the influence. From behind, three white men in a pick-up truck followed James closely. In the trial later, at least one of the men was found to be a white supremacist. And because they did not monitor and watch their hate odometers, all three men beat James Byrd, Jr. savagely. Then, they slashed his throat, sprayed him with black spray paint and chained him to the back of the pick-up truck and drove, dragging his body for approximately three miles.

Hate didn't just arrive at the scene that day. Their seeds of bitterness and intolerance had been planted and cultivated until they blossomed and escalated into full-fledged hate. These men's hate had grown so intense and deep that when they detached his body from the pick-up truck, Mr. Byrd's head was decapitated from his shoulders and a left arm was torn from his frame as well. Finished with him, they callously dumped Mr. Byrd's maimed body in front of a predominately black church in town.

Young, Gay and Murdered

Another tragic case occurring in Laramie, Wyoming, provides another example of unchecked and unmonitored hate odometers gone out of control. Matthew Shepard was gay and on the night of October 6, 1998, two men pretending to be gay lured Matt from the Fireside Lounge. Once Matt was in the car with them, they drove him to a remote location. There they tied him to a fence, tortured, beat and pistol-whipped him with the butt of a .357 Magnum until he was almost dead. When police found him, Matthew Shepard's entire face was covered with blood, except for areas washed white from his tears. He died after languishing in a coma for approximately four days. Matthew was a 21-year-old college student who was brutally murdered because of his sexual orientation due to the diversity hate, fear and ignorance of two homophobic men.

In these two instances, hate odometers were not being watched, checked or monitored. Hate, manifested through violent rage, fueled out-of-control behavior in the men and provoked them to do bodily harm to their victims. Ultimately, this rage resulted in the beastly murders of James Byrd, Jr. and Matthew Shepard. The deep-rooted hate of race and sexual orientation transformed these men into murderers. Unlike the men who murdered these individuals, most people think they would never allow their feelings about diversity conflict and tension to get out of control and escalate into hate, violent rage or hate and bias-motivated crimes.

You may never inflict the kinds of physical pain onto another human being like what happened to James Byrd Jr. and Matthew Shepard. But, you might be responsible for killing someone's professional career if you fire her or him unfairly because of an unchecked and unmonitored hate odometer. What if you refused to hire or promote someone because of your Diversity BAPS? Would you call that career assassination? I would! Would you call it lifestyle or viability assassination? I would!

If you are a loan officer at a bank, you might kill their ability to purchase a home. As a finance manager at an automobile dealership, you might kill their ability to finance a car. Allowing your hate odometer to run unchecked does not mean you will murder a person physically, but you might defeat and destroy them in other ways. And, though you may not kill someone through physical and aggressive means, you may kill a person through abuse and misuse of a position of power and influence or by destroying and killing a person's dreams, goals and aspirations. This makes it imperative that each of us, whatever our profession or work or school environment, watch our hate odometer and Diversity BAPS, so we do not allow our own emotions to dominate and get the best of us.

FIRE - The Diversity Barrier of Ignorance

Having a lack of diversity knowledge or being diversity ignorant about the different dimensions of diversity is a common barrier to diversity competence. However, it is a barrier that we can easily overcome. Acquiring diversity knowledge and gaining diversity exposure and experience through communicating and interacting with diverse people can help you overcome ignorance. Caution: this is *not* a barrier to be ashamed of. As Will Rogers once said, "We are all *ignorant*, only on different subjects."

Ignorance and Lack of Exposure

Diversity ignorance may be due to a *lack of exposure*, either by choice or by sheer demographics. For example, if you happened to grow up in a small, homogenous community with a population where all the people are the same, it is entirely possible you would not have experienced diverse people, other cultures, religions, languages, foods, customs and practices. As a result, you could personally choose to remain in that environment and never develop experiential diversity knowledge about people different from those around you. However, you may decide to learn about and experience aspects of diversity your formative years *never* allowed or provided.

In some cases, demographics may forestall the need for diversity education. Like in many farming and rural communities in the U.S., what if businesses in your small, comfortable town start hiring immigrants to work in industrial or agricultural jobs that many Americans disregard? If immigrants begin moving into the community with their extended families and children, their new diversity will greatly impact how the community functions and operates. In no time at all, your homogeneous community could find itself in need of an ELL (English Language Leaner) program in the schools. The local hospital, police and 9-1-1 emergency systems would need to accommodate the new diversity as well by offering bilingual options. Additionally, businesses might choose to have bilingual signage and offer other product assortments to support the new diversity in the community. In short, diversity comes to you whether you are ready for it or not.

Ignorance and Lack of Experience

Ignorance about diversity can also be due to a *lack of experience*. A diversity experience implies that an individual possesses first-hand diversity knowledge regarding a person, culture or diverse community based on personal encounters and interpersonal observations.

Dr. Mary-Frances Winters writes about the importance of gaining more diversity experiences and encounters in her book *Inclusion Starts with I,* in which she states,

> *"Learning about others is a life-long journey of experiences. It is not enough to say, "I know one of them" or "One of my best friends is_____" and think you understand another culture. This leads us to narrow, stereotypical views. Reading about, traveling to, engaging with other cultures is the best way to really truly learn about others.*
>
> *When we open ourselves to learning about others, we learn more about ourselves. Learning about others shows us how we are connected as a human race and opens the possibilities for collaboration and cooperation rather than competition.*
>
> *Our workplaces force us to interact with others. Our communities do not. We still live primarily in ethnically segregated enclaves. As individuals, you can choose to expand your knowledge of others. If enough of us make such a commitment, we will move towards an inclusive world."*

Putting ourselves in new situations to experience new types of cultures and individuals is another step in your journey to becoming diversity competent.

I, too, have had to challenge myself to take a risk and overcome my personal ignorance of diverse people. For example, I was deathly afraid and felt interpersonally awkward and diversity incompetent when I attended Elmhurst College, and I had my first diversity encounter and experience with Nobuhiro Nishitani, an international student from Japan. I did not know how to act, nor did I know what to say when we first met. It was as if I viewed myself as normal and Nobuhiro as abnormal. Once again, in my mind, I was a human, and I perceived him as an extraterrestrial being from another planet. At age seventeen, I was very ignorant of different ethnicities and I referred to all Asians as Chinese, so I did not even know Nobuhiro was

Japanese until he explained his cultural and ethnic background to me.

A move to a more diverse geographic area might place you in a complex and confusing environment temporarily—much more different than the geography you are most comfortable with. You may feel unsure of which communication style to use and/or not to use. If you can handle this initial point of diversity discomfort, you will gain great diversity experience in this kind of environment, and will be able to take away an immeasurable amount of confidence, which will bring you closer to becoming diversity competent.

Ignorance and Lack of Education

Even the most confident individuals, when communicating and interacting with diverse people, can lack adequate education and information on certain diversity topics. A *lack of education* impacts diversity competence on many levels. Doing your diversity homework to become knowledgeable of diverse cultures and diverse issues is critical to becoming diversity competent. A diversity education can be formal, such as enrolling in classes and seminars regarding a particular cultural or ethnic group, or the education can be informal, such as deciding to participate in culturally diverse events or organizations.

Self-education affords a great opportunity to expand your understanding of diverse cultures. And whatever way you choose to educate yourself about diversity will bring you great rewards.

From Ignorance to Education: The GLBT Friendly Mother

I know a mother named Pam who attended a Gay PRIDE Parade with her adult lesbian daughter Paula. The diversity experience and encounter at the Gay PRIDE Parade for Pam was highly educational, informational and eye opening. Was Pam apprehensive about going to the PRIDE Parade when Paula initially invited her to go? Absolutely she was! Did Pam experience diversity anxiety and discomfort before, during and after the visit to the PRIDE Parade with Paula? Yes, yes and yes indeed! However, Pam began the process of a diversity education by willingly attending the PRIDE

Parade to learn more about Paula's sexual orientation and the issues surrounding the GLBT community. By attending the PRIDE Parade, Pam was able to ask "GLBT questions" in an objective and non-threatening environment at the various tables and booths.

It was at this event that Pam initially embarked upon a diversity journey to learn more about the GLBT community, because of her daughter. However, after attending the PRIDE Parade, it stimulated and motivated Pam to conduct a diversity quest to learn more about her daughter Paula and the GLBT community. After six months of personal and interpersonal diversity exploration, I am proud to say that Pam joined PFLAG (Parents, Families and Friends of Lesbians and Gays) as a continuation of her diversity quest and in support of her loving daughter Paula.

FI**R**E - The Diversity Barrier of Resentment

Resentment, Affirmative Action and Reverse Discrimination

Perceptual differences over extremely controversial political and social issues have been a HUGE barrier in society, leaving us with a nation of diversity incompetent individuals and organizations. Divisive issues over emotional topics have been the barriers to diversity competence for many. Whether it is the workplace or one of the many academic institutions, issues of *Affirmative Action* and *reverse discrimination* are very real. These programs and others create, not only resentment among the parties involved, but can also lead to an individual becoming hardened and more close-minded around diversity in general. Often resentment leads to a person developing a "lose-lose" or a "win-lose" mentality rather than a "compromise" or a "win-win" mentality. This kind of resentment can easily lead to anger and irritation and eventually hatred toward another individual or a diverse group of people.

In order to help combat this issue, in Affirmative Action programs, women and people of color are given greater overall odds of obtaining a job or an admissions approval in order for schools or workplaces to increase diversity. The flipside of

Affirmative Action is that those not represented in the gender or racial minority can feel discriminated against by these programs (most often white males). One example of this took place in a county-level organization where an attempt was made to increase the number of women and people of color probation officers. The white male probation officers, who were the majority at the organization, currently working there (some for many years) became upset, angered and concerned about their own chances for promotion and upward mobility. While there was a clear advantage to having women and people of color probation officers given the racial background of many offenders, the white males became close-minded to that fact and were only concerned about their jobs and the possibility of not advancing into leadership roles and positions rather than ensuring gender and racial equality.

Affirmative Action: Is it Right or is it Wrong? (The Great Diversity Debate)

Affirmative Action is praised and hated, celebrated and tolerated and commended and rebuked by its proponents and opponents. Whether at a college campus or corporate organization, I find Affirmative Action as one of the most divisive issues today, often creating gender and racial hostility and diversity tension and preventing people from becoming diversity competent.

Why are there so many emotions and diversity conflicts over the issue of Affirmative Action? That question naturally leads us back to a racially chaotic time in U.S. history. Introduced and signed into law in 1965 by President Lyndon B. Johnson, the Affirmative Action law was a proactive and positive attempt to eliminate past and present practices of discrimination against people of color. The original goal of Affirmative Action was to correct the inequalities and injustices of the past due to legalized privileges for white Americans. The original intent was not to personally and professionally destroy white males, but to rectify America's destructive past of racial inequality within organizations and schools.

However, the other side is that the implementation of Affirmative Action fuels white critics' cries of 'reverse discrimination.' The concept of reverse discrimination is a reaction to the policy to correct the discrimination of women and people of color. Objection to the policy is based on the belief that opportunities are lost by mainly white males when given to women and people of color as mandated by Affirmative Action law.

I have found that the subject of Affirmative Action creates diversity conflict and tension whenever I am in organizations, schools and other environments. White men say, "People of color and women benefit at our expense." White men continue to say, "We're robbed of opportunities and job promotions" and "Affirmative Action opens doors for people of color but closes doors on whites."

Conversely, people of color—particularly African-Americans—say, "Considering America's horrible treatment of us, especially during slavery, it's about time they owned up to the injustices that took place." African-Americans continue to say, "We see Affirmative Action as a good thing because it levels the playing field. It gives us access and opportunities to areas we have been typically barred and historically prohibited from partaking in." They add, "It is not the answer to past injustices, but it is an ambitious attempt to do the right thing—to mend racial relationships that were historically broken and destroyed."

When proponents of Affirmative Action hear about the backlash and talk of repealing the law, it infuriates people of color more. They point out, "Once people of color start to advance, white males don't like it and that's why they're complaining." They feel this sort of talk indicates that America's resolve toward the issue is questionable, adding, "So, America is not as serious as we thought they were regarding leveling the playing field for ALL people. They don't want to do the right thing." And, these feelings foster more diversity resentment and lead to more diversity conflict and tension.

Defending their cries of reverse discrimination, some white men reply, "I didn't own any slaves. My family isn't rich. I went to college and pulled myself up by my bootstraps to get where I've gotten. I have a family; I have a mortgage and bills to pay. Now, I've lost my career opportunity because of Affirmative Action. I'm angry, and I hate Affirmative Action. It is morally unfair." Whites on college campuses think blacks lessen their opportunities, saying, "Every time I see a student of color, I think they're here because of Affirmative Action."

The above opinions surfaced during a presentation to a group of probation officers. The organization could not move forward because of the diversity anger and resentment evoked by the conflicting issues of Affirmative Action and reverse discrimination. The white male probation officers gave all of the reasons listed above for their anger—and more. The people of color replied, "But every time there's an opportunity to hire diverse candidates that are competent and qualified, you keep hiring the same type of people—white men—not even white women."

It is True the Issue of Affirmative Action is Very Divisive

People sometimes ask, "Jermaine, how do you feel about both issues?" I respond by saying, "In an ideal world, people would do the right thing all the time. I believe people should be just and fair; they should avoid stereotyping or allowing their Diversity BAPS (Biases, Assumptions, Prejudices and Stereotypes) to determine how they will communicate and interact with diverse people. In an ideal world, people *would* do the right thing. But, we don't live in an ideal world, and because people willingly submit to their Diversity BAPS, they do not always do the right thing. So, I understand why Lyndon B. Johnson in 1965, signed this significant document into law."

I truly believe it is not the churches, corporations, government agencies and schools that discriminate, but rather the people in those buildings that perform the acts of injustice and inequality. If everyone in leadership roles, positions of influence and positions of power hated and despised unfairness, there would be no need for Affirmative Action. In fact, if this were the case, there would be no need for me to write this section discussing this as one of the barriers to becoming diversity competent. Unfortunately, we cannot mandate that people do the right thing because it does not work. Emotions cannot be regulated. Cognitive thoughts cannot be regulated. Years ago, Gandhi observed, "Prejudices cannot be removed by legislation." Until people start doing the right thing, we will continue to have acts of discrimination based on age, disability, race, gender, sexual orientation and religious preference. This reality necessitates a law such as the Affirmative Action law. What else can we do? How else can we guarantee people will stop discriminating? How else do we ensure that women and people of color are not excluded simply because they are not a part of the good ole' boy network?

Affirmative Action is an ambitious attempt to right a wrong and to correct a historical problem that desperately needs attention. In an ideal world, it would not be needed. But, in the real world, I understand why it is needed. It is a necessary law with pros and cons, benefits and liabilities, positives and negatives, smiles and tears. I say, let us eliminate Affirmative Action, but we must first guarantee justice, equality and fairness for ALL people.

> "Racism is when you have laws set up, systematically put in a way to keep people from advancing, to stop the advancement of a people. Black people have never had the power to enforce racism, and so this is something that white America is going to have to work out themselves. If they decide they want to stop it, curtail it, or to do the right thing...then it will be done, but not until then."
> **Spike Lee**

Other Issues Complicating Diversity Competence

Resentment and Gender Issues

Gender resentment. Gender conflict. What am I talking about? There is no gender tension between women and men in the workplace anymore! I mean, aren't women of equal status now? Yes, there are more women in corporate positions than ever before, more women-owned businesses than ever before and more women making greater strides than ever before. However, there are still major workplace issues that foster workplace conflict, tension and resentment among female and male colleagues. Women with the same education and work experience as men continue to lag behind their male colleagues in wages. There continues to be inequities in job assignments and responsibilities in the workplace. Sadly, the perception exists in subtle ways implying that men are naturally born to be leaders and bread-winners among the genders.

Evelyn Murphy, author of the book, *Getting Even: Why Women Don't Get Paid Like Men—and What to Do About It*, says of gender pay inequities, "Over her working lifetime, a woman will lose between $700,000 and $2 million." Whether real or perceived, gender-based workplace issues such as job assignment inequalities, pay inequities, the glass ceiling phenomenon and the relationship between career advancement and sexual harassment in male-dominated industries and organizations can prevent both women and men from becoming diversity competent. Women and men both express annoyingly, when gender-based issues lead to societal and workplace conflict, "Here we go again." In others words, "Aren't we done with these issues?" My reply is, "Apparently not," as long as there are apparent gender-based injustices and inequities still occurring within organizations today.

Workplace discrimination based on gender is a deeply-rooted issue entrenched in America's past transgressions of sexism. America's bravado of male dominance has a deep history of being unfair and unkind to women. Yes, there are many men who are NOT sexist and they advocate for women's equality, rights and issues, but the biggest challenge is defeating covert and deep-rooted attitudes that lead to gender-based discrimination and inequities. Men in male-dominated organizations and industries must be deliberate about creating work environments where women feel included and welcome. Men must be intentional with regard to integrating women into the regular rhythm of the male-dominated environment. If women do not feel included, many will assume that the best workplace opportunities are still designated for men.

Men who have a difficult time understanding women's workplace issues and challenges often ask these kinds of questions:

- Don't we have more women as board members than ever before?

- Aren't more women running small, medium and large corporations than in the past?

- Doesn't research and statistics show more females start small businesses in the United States than men?

- Hasn't there been an increase of female politicians being elected to office over the last two decades?

I reply to their questions using the response of the game show host of Family Feud when a contestant correctly answers a question by stating, "Survey says, yes!" Yes, statistically speaking, there has been an increase of female participation and involvement in business and the marketplace in general. However, my follow-up question is more of a rhetorical question when I ask, "Just because there's more female participation and involvement within businesses and the marketplace, does that imply male-dominated organizations and industries have completely welcomed women with open arms?"

I learned from working with leaders, employees and students representing all dimensions of diversity from around the U.S., that an invitation to participate does not guarantee inclusion. ***Inclusion is embracing and welcoming a newcomer's individuality and diversity until she or he is made a part of the environment.*** Imagine I invite you to my house for dinner. Does my invitation ensure that I will treat you kindly, warmly and respectfully? We would hope that a guest receiving an invitation would be treated with the utmost respect. However, white male-dominated organizations and industries have to be very deliberate and intentional about being great hosts when they invite women into their traditionally male-dominated organizations and industries if they want women to be and feel included. I do not mean they should patronize women, but include them deliberately and intentionally.

Resentment and White Privilege

"Pull yourself up by your bootstraps and anyone, and I mean anyone can become somebody in America." Is this a valid statement or is it a far cry from reality? Can everyone really make it in America? Is this statement filled with ridiculous platitudes? Do all ethnic and racial groups really have the same opportunities as everyone else? Are there certain ethnic and racial groups that are bestowed with more privileges, opportunities and granted more leniency than other ethnic and racial groups in the U.S.? Does justice, equality, fairness and freedom really exist for all people in America? Does racism and sexism really exist in the U.S. or is it a figment of our imagination?

It has been said that the formula for success in America is hard work and dedication, and anyone can make it. Does the United States of America have a history of playing favoritism based on skin preference and privilege? Is there *any* possibility that institutional and systemic racism could keep hard working and dedicated people of color from achieving the American dream? Yes indeed!

America has historically favored the diversity that represents its founding fathers: white men. This is not an attack on or against white men—this is a reality. When this great country was founded and established by white men, the original framework and foundation did not include the values, concerns and issues of diverse people. It mirrored the values, concerns and issues of the founding fathers, who were ALL white men.

Headlines in a plethora of magazines and newspapers reveal that many people of color still suffer from skin discrimination. An article in the *Chicago Sun-Times* entitled, "Suit: Chrysler denied loans to blacks," reveals that skin color privilege and skin color disadvantage definitely plays a HUGE role in determining the plight of certain ethnic and racial groups within the United States. The *Chicago Sun-Times* wrote:

> *"Daimler Chrysler denied low interest car loans to customers because they were black and employed a financing manager, who regularly spewed racial epithets...Six African Americans from the Chicago area sued the fifth largest automaker, alleging they were victims of redlining and were recently turned down for Chrysler loans at a South Side dealership...The customers had received high marks for their credit histories but had to get loans with higher interest rates at other financial institutions.*
>
> *In addition, about 70 cars purchased through the dealership, mainly by African Americans who did get their loans from Chrysler, had their vehicles improperly repossessed once a zone manager responsible for financing learned of the race of the people getting the loans, the suit says.*
>
> *According to the lawsuit, a zone manager (who is not referred to by name in the suit), explained why African Americans weren't entitled to car loans in one conversation with managers, commenting: "Do you really believe that these people really think that they should have a new car? These people shouldn't be able to get financed for a Schwinn (bicycle). Those n------ have never paid anyone.*

The zone manager said he would allow "some n------" to take out loans at suburban dealerships "because at least they're smart enough not to get shot while trying to buy a car in the ghetto."

This is merely one story and one example of race-based and skin-based discrimination that caught my attention while researching and writing *Be Diversity Competent*. There are millions of stories that illustrate that we still live, work and play in a color-conscious and race-based society. To deny this reality, which often happens, only leads to more diversity conflict and tension in life, school and work. Acknowledging that this reality exists communicates personal and professional maturity, and it is paramount to the reduction of diversity hostility and resentment that still exists within America's communities, houses of faith and worship, organizations and schools.

So what is this reality that so many people refuse to acknowledge and deny its existence, which causes an abundance of diversity conflict, tension and resentment? It is called "white privilege." **White privilege is a conscious and/ or unconscious advantage or benefit experienced and enjoyed by white people in life, school and work.** You may be thinking to yourself, who granted white Americans this so-called privilege? The United States government deliberately and systematically granted white Americans preferential treatment through its laws, policies, practices and procedures. People of color were deliberately and systemically denied fair and equal treatment. People of color were systematically denied access to quality employment, education, health and housing. Previous U.S. laws, policies, practices and procedures, which favored white Americans over people of color, are hugely responsible for the social injustices and economic inequalities we presently see in American culture today.

> "It is the mark of an educated mind to be able to entertain a thought without accepting it."
> **Aristotle**

The white privilege school of thought does not believe, teach or imply that all white people are evil, racist, hate mongers, filthy rich, bad or immoral people. Educating others on white privilege informs people of the favoritism granted to white people in America because of their skin color. White privilege does not mean that white people do not have to get up every day and go to work.

That would be a ridiculous assumption to make or believe. The fact that I see white people going to and coming from work every day dismantles the entire assumption white people do not have to work because of white privilege. If that were the case, there would only be a handful of people showing up to work on a daily basis. Of course, white people have to work and yes, they have to work hard and diligent as well. However, white privilege educates, informs and raises the awareness of how white skin is highly favored and in some places, preferred over other kinds of skin tones and complexions.

You may be thinking to yourself, "Come on Jermaine. I know you are not playing the race card game to try and explain the differences between those who have and those who have not." Perhaps you may be thinking, "I've worked hard to achieve everything I've acquired in life, school and work." Let me start by saying I would never, ever maliciously or intentionally demean, devalue or disrespect a white female or male by making a ridiculous assumption that ALL their achievements and accomplishments were attained because of their skin color. That colossal and insidious statement would greatly contradict my personal and professional beliefs regarding personal and professional accountability and responsibility.

However, I do believe that white privilege in the United States of America has been very advantageous and beneficial to those with white skin. I believe it would be ridiculous for anyone to deny and refute that white privilege and skin preference is a wonderful asset to have while navigating through a highly color-conscious society. Having white skin in the U.S. does not imply that a white person's life is a piece of cake. As my grandmother would say, "That would be a boldface lie and far from the truth." Simply stated, life is just a little bit easier if your skin tone and complexion mirrors that of the majority and of the founding fathers of this great nation—the United States of America.

The following examples of white privilege are based on the original work of Peggy McIntosh's 1988 groundbreaking essay entitled, "White Privilege: Unpacking the Invisible Knapsack":

So what is white privilege, exactly (consider the following examples of white privilege)?

- When seeking to rent an apartment or purchase a home, white people can pretty much count on not being discriminated against because of their skin color.

- White people can be pretty sure that their new neighbors will be either pleasant, welcoming or at minimum, cordial towards them.

- White people can go shopping alone most of the time and not have to worry about being followed, harassed or suspected as a shoplifter.

- White people don't have to worry about being discriminated against because they sound like a person of color or "too ethnic."

- White people can turn on the television or open the newspaper and see white people widely respected and represented in a positive manner.

- White people can be assured that their children will be taught from an educational curriculum that testifies and reinforces the existence of their race, which does not happen very often with people of color in school settings.

- White people don't have to consistently educate their children on racism and sensitive diversity-related issues for their own mental, emotional and physical well-being and safety.

- In learning environments, white people can pretty much be assured they will learn how other white people have made significant contributions in the United States of America.

- White people can count on their skin color not working against them when making purchases with checks, credit cards, money orders or cash.

- White people don't have to worry about being asked to speak for or give an opinion that explains all the white people in America.

- White people don't have to wonder if a police officer pulled their car over or stopped them on the street because of the color of their skin.

- White people can take a job with an Affirmative Action employer without having colleagues and co-workers on the job suspect they got the job because of their race.

- White people can be assured that if legal or medical help is needed, their race will not work against them.

- White people don't have to worry about racially being accepted or "fitting in" when starting a new job or attending a new school.

- White people don't have to wonder if their skin color will determine if they get approved for a bank loan.

- White people don't have to worry about if their colleagues will have a difficult time being managed or led by them because of their skin color.

- White people can often see other white people in all levels of the organization.

These examples illustrate just a few of the advantages and benefits enjoyed and experienced by white people in life, school and work. Some white people deny the notion and existence of white privilege. It is difficult for some white people to recognize and understand the advantages and benefits of white privilege from a person of color's perspective. The difficulty is rooted in the American success and achievement model, which states, "Pull Yourself Up by Your Boot Straps." This paradigm teaches that anyone can become successful in America by working hard and being dedicated. It is implied that all people are granted the same opportunities and it is an individual's choices that determine their amount and level of success in life, school and work. This model of success and achievement works extremely well when race is *not* a factor.

Historically, people of color have been excluded from and denied access to opportunities in the areas of banking, education, employment, housing and politics due to the color of their skin. Those with white skin have been privileged throughout American history to enjoy and experience the above mentioned opportunities. Typically, people of color can spot white privilege very easily and quickly because they know what it is like to live in and work in a nation where your skin color, tone and complexion is not favored and celebrated. In other words, there are disadvantages to not having white skin in a color and race-conscious nation. The notion of white privilege whether you agree it exists or not, is a major thorn in America's side because it causes diversity resentment, and it definitely prevents many individuals and organizations from becoming diversity competent.

When I conduct diversity workshops, I often ask the attendees, "What are the key diversity barriers that prevent healthy diversity dialogues and discussions from occurring on your campus or within your organization?" The audience members who are courageous enough to put the real issues on the table will often reply, "One of the key barriers is the divisive issue of white privilege (sometimes interchangeably referred to as "systemic racism" and "institutional racism"). In other words, people of color who are employees of predominantly white organizations and students of color at predominantly white colleges and universities often receive pushback when they bring up the emotionally charged issue of white privilege, systemic racism or institutional racism. They run the risk of hearing negative comments and pushback statements such as:

- "Here we go again with that racism stuff."

- "Can't we all just get along?"

- "There is no racism here. It's racism because you make it racism. Racism is a figment of your imagination."

- "We all have to work hard in America to get ahead. Just pull yourself up by your bootstraps and you can be successful just like the rest of us."

- "Why are you playing the race card?"

- "We're all the same color on the inside."

- "We all get the same choices, freedoms and opportunities in life and America."

- "Get over it! Why are we still dealing with this stuff?"

When people of color hear these kinds or similar kinds of statements from white people regarding their perceptions of race-related issues and conflicts, it makes people of color feel as if their diversity-related experiences, encounters and perceptions have no validity. Diversity chaos, conflict and tension begins to build intensely when diverse colleagues, employees and students housed in predominantly white environments begin to feel as if their diversity-related experiences are demeaned, devalued, discredited, disrespected and denied.

Meritocracy: Fact or Fiction?

Meritocracy is the idealistic belief that a person is able to get ahead in life and in the workplace on the basis of her or his own merits. Using meritocracy in the workplace, for example, would mean that at the time of hiring or a promotion, logical and unbiased steps are taken to determine the individual who best merits the position or the promotion.

Unfortunately, fair and equitable employment practices are not always abided by as they should. People emotionally favor one person over others. An employee can be an employee who does great work and possesses a great work ethic, and she or he can still be passed over for a job promotion because a manager or a leader does not personally like them or their unique diversity. This behavior totally destroys the ideal and philosophy of meritocracy. There is nepotism in the workplace, especially in smaller companies that are family-owned. In the real world, people have Diversity BAPS (Biases, Assumptions, Prejudices and Stereotypes) that interfere with their decision-making.

Can one conceive of a world based on meritocracy? How would it change the workplace environment? Would the manager's sister or brother work harder, so that she or he could rightfully earn the promotion? Will the person who stays in the background and works extremely hard at their job be able to move up in the management ranks without having to deal with corporate politics? Can we exist in a world without Diversity BAPS affecting our decision-making?

As ideal as meritocracy sounds, it is important for individuals and organizations to understand that not all people get ahead in life, school and work because of their own efforts, but many get ahead because they are favored and also because of nepotism.

FIRE - The Diversity Barrier of Ego

Egocentrism

A healthy ego monitored and checked often is not necessarily negative unless it interferes with your goal of diversity competence. *Egocentrism,* however, reveals itself through thoughts like, "I am superior to you." This feeling of ego superiority becomes a problem because the counterpart to "I am superior to you" becomes "You are inferior to me." Such a perceived difference automatically puts two people on different levels of quality and value—something not conducive to diversity competence. The egocentric individual has a tendency to overvalue their worth while devaluing the worth of the individual that they perceive they are better than. An egocentric paradigm is definitely a barrier when communicating and interacting with diverse people. When an egocentric individual is conversing with someone that she or he believes they are superior to, they are more likely to disrespect the person by abruptly interrupting them or harshly talking down to them. Here are some examples of egocentrism:

- I am heterosexual, and I believe I am better than gays.

- I am male, and I believe I am better than women.

- I am white, and I believe I am better than people of color.

- I am a Christian, and I believe I am better than Muslims.

Ethnocentrism

Do you believe your way of doing things is the only correct and right way of doing things? Do you see your ethnic group or cultural practices as superior to those of other ethnic groups and cultural practices? Do you judge other groups who are completely different from your group according to the standards and values of your own group? If you answered "yes" to any of the previous questions, you are highly likely to practice ethnocentrism when communicating and interacting with diverse cultures and people.

Ethnocentrism is the attitude and belief that one's own culture and race is superior to other cultures and races. The ethnocentric person says, "I see *us* as better and *them* as worse." Ethnocentrism occurs intentionally and unintentionally, consciously and unconsciously while communicating and interacting with others who are different from you. For example, pretend I am an American who disregards the cultural standards of people from other countries, and I judge them according to American standards and values. In America, pursuing higher education for high school graduates is an overall American value; however, there are immigrants and refugees who come to America, and they may pursue taking care of their immediate family and extended families by obtaining employment before enrolling in college. If I have talked negatively about or put down an immigrant or refugee for not immediately enrolling into school when they arrive in America, then I have behaved in an ethnocentric manner.

Ethnocentrism is a major barrier to becoming diversity competent because an ethnocentric viewpoint is closely related to arrogance, close-mindedness and self-righteousness. Ethnocentric individuals believe that they are right and others are wrong, especially if they do not hold and honor their perspectives or worldviews. Ethnocentric individuals tend to believe that other parts of the world should share the exact same ideologies, philosophies, morals, perspectives and worldviews as their own. The diversity conflict and tension begins when there are diversity encounters, and diverse people do not act and behave as we think they should.

It is quite normal to feel pride in your ethnic origin and in some cases, to feel that the way your ethnic group does things is the "best way" or "only way" things should be done. If you happen to live in a community where there is only one dominant ethnic group, you may not even be aware of the customs and practices of other ethnic groups until you encounter them.

The "my culture is better than yours" attitude is a destructive attitude to possess. The important thing to remember is that having cultural and ethnic pride is possible without belittling, devaluing, disregarding and disrespecting the cultural practices, beliefs and characteristics of other cultures or demanding that others adapt to your cultural style. If you fail to see the *benefits* and *contributions* that other cultures and ethnic group can offer, you are more likely to be considered ethnocentric and fail to see that there may be other ways of doing things than what you have become accustomed to.

The exact opposite of ethnocentrism is referred to as "Ethnorelativism" or sometimes called "cultural relativism" by cultural anthropologists. Milton J. Bennett, editor of the book, *Basic Concepts of Intercultural Communication*, ***defines ethnorelativism as, "...Being comfortable with many standards and customs and...having an ability to adapt behavior and judgments to a variety of interpersonal settings."*** Ethnorelativism and cultural relativism have both positive and negative dimensions and should be explored respectfully as one seeks diversity competence.

Professor and anthropologist Dr. Conrad P. Kottak, describes the pros and cons of cultural relativism in his book *Cultural Anthropology* when he writes, "Cultural relativism is the argument that behavior in a particular culture should not be judged by the standards of another. This position can also present problems. At its most extreme, cultural relativism argues that there is no superior, international or universal morality, that the moral and ethical rules of all cultures deserve equal respect."

So, which behavior will you practice while communicating and interacting with diverse people—cultural relativism or ethnocentrism? Please choose wisely!

My Skin is My Sin (The Sammy Story)

I was invited to give a compelling 75-minute keynote presentation entitled, "Exploring Diversity: The Art of Understanding and Getting Along with Diverse People," during orientation week at a prestigious school in upstate New York. There were approximately 1,500 audience members consisting of first-year and transfer college students, professional staff, faculty and college administrators.

After completing the exhausting keynote, I began packing my suitcase with the various visual aids I used during my presentation. Periodically someone would stop to shake my hand, chat for a minute or tell me how much she or he appreciated the presentation. One young man in particular stepped boldly onto the stage, clasped my hand in his own, and introduced himself as Sammy.

Sammy shared how much he loved the presentation, and that he had learned a lot about being diversity competent as a college student and future international business entrepreneur. Sammy said he had a burning question for me. With a sincere glint in his eye, he asked, "What should I do when I try to make friends as a new college student and other students won't accept and embrace me?"

I looked at him and said, "Well, what's wrong with you? Why wouldn't someone want to be friends with you? I don't understand." I gave him a quick look over from head to toe and continued, "You look like a handsome young fellow to me, and you were quite cordial and respectful when you approached me!"

Sammy said, "I'm from Kuwait." He appeared very proud of his nationality.

I replied, "And your point is what, Sammy?"

Sammy was dark-haired with a dark olive-skin tone and complexion. His facial features ethnically appeared to resemble someone geographically from a Middle Eastern country. I knew that "post-9/11" Sammy was implying he could not make college friends because of how students perceived him (as a potential terrorist).

Sammy's ethnic characteristics, along with his olive-colored skin tone and complexion were interfering with his ability to establish and build friendships on a predominantly white college campus. I knew he was looking to me to affirm his beliefs, but I wanted Sammy to verbally acknowledge why he thought he was being stereotyped and prejudged. He was being excluded because he was not a part of what sociologists and intercultural specialists refer to as the "ingroup."

In the book, *Readings on Communicating with Strangers*, authors William Gudykunst and Young Yun Kim distinguish between ingroups and outgroups when they write, "Our ingroups are groups which we identify as important to us. When we interact with another person, we categorize that person as being a member of an ingroup or an outgroup. We experience more uncertainty and anxiety when we communicate with members of outgroups than when we communicate with members of ingroups."

Sammy's facial expression communicated sadness, and his voice filled with defeat as he explained, "With a big smile on my face, I cordially walk up to other students and introduce myself, share my major with them to try to establish some sort of common bond and say 'Hello' while walking through the hallways and residence halls; students either avoid me, ignore me or simply turn away from me."

As he spoke, I immediately became emotionally distraught. I thought to myself, this diversity incompetence has got to stop; it is destroying us as a people. I literally felt helpless and hopeless. I felt sad for Sammy and his diversity-related predicament. His story brought tears to my eyes. I could relate to Sammy's experience because I was in Sammy's same shoes when I attended undergraduate and graduate school at Elmhurst College, the University of Wisconsin-Superior and Saint Mary's University. It is, in fact, my own diversity-related experiences like Sammy's that compelled and motivated me to aggressively continue my diversity-related work as a teacher, speaker and writer; still, his situation deeply saddened my spirit. I knew if people did not embrace Sammy, his college career and future would be a bleak one in the U.S. I knew his diversity conflict and tension could drive him to quit school and to leave the U.S. carrying negative impressions and perceptions of Americans.

Through a series of rhetorical questions, I shared this with him, "Sammy, what if I told you that there are some people on this campus who are stereotyping, prejudging and labeling you as a potential terrorist? Do you believe there are students who really want to get to know you, but out of fear, ignorance and being diversity incompetent, they simply choose to avoid or ignore you altogether?"

Sammy looked perplexed for a moment before asking, "So people probably think I'm a terrorist and, oh, let me guess, they probably think I'm somehow related to Osama Bin Laden and Saddam Hussein, right?"

I replied, "Unfortunately, Sammy, we live in a world where people stereotype, prejudge and make assumptions about diverse people 24 hours a day, seven days a week and 365 days a year, without personally getting to know the people they are stereotyping and prejudging."

Sammy, looking defeated, replied, "That is very wrong, Jermaine! It's morally wrong to judge a book by its cover. I wish people would get to know me and give me a fair chance before they stereotype and prejudge me."

I replied, "I agree Sammy. I wish people would give you a fair chance before stereotyping and prejudging you according to your ethnic profile, skin tone and complexion."

Sammy asked me with a smirk on his face, "Do you think I'm a terrorist?"

I turned his question back to him, responding "Are you a terrorist?"

Sammy replied, "No."

I smiled, and said, "That's what I thought, but I thought I'd better ask just in case you had a little secret you wanted to share with me."

As I left the auditorium Sammy walked me to my rental car, and we laughed together because the thought of him being a terrorist seemed ridiculous. Then, I said, "I assumed you were not a terrorist." I added, "People fear and avoid what they do not understand. And, they fear you and prejudge you because your physical attributes and ethnic resemblance reminds them of the images they see on television of the nineteen men who were responsible for the September 11, 2001 attack and atrocity. They are looking at your physical composition, making decisions whether or not to include or exclude you." I said, "Sammy, as the rapper, turned actor, director and movie producer Ice Cube says, "Your skin is your sin."

Unfortunately, Sammy was carrying the unbearable burden and paying the all too expensive price of not being the right color on his college campus. There are many Sammys in organizations carrying that same burden and paying the same price as well. How unfortunate! If Sammy were your classmate, colleague, neighbor or a member of your house of faith or worship, what advice would you give him?

■   ■   ■

Part 4

Diversity
Skills

In the first three parts of the book, we explored many difficulties individuals and organizations face when dealing with diversity including diversity avoidance, diversity denial and diversity minimization. In part four, we will delve deeply into practicing diversity skills to improve interpersonal communication with diverse people. The three diversity competent skills are: Attitudinal, Behavioral and Communicative. These skills offer individuals and organizations a variety of examples and techniques, which help to reduce diversity conflict and tension. For example, personal stories, professional scenarios and exercises can be used as a resource to help you recognize how diversity is affecting you and your organization and what you can do about it.

The long-term objective of acquiring diversity competent skills is to develop self-confidence. This confidence will help you when communicating and interacting with diverse people. The communication and diversity skills provided in this book are tools to assist you in correcting diversity-related problems when you encounter them. These tools will help you build better relationships with diverse people. Implementing and practicing the various diversity skills offered in *Be Diversity Competent* will give you tremendous courage over your diversity anxiety, fear and uneasiness. Please take notes and reflect as you read and study the three diversity competent skills.

Attitudinal Skills

An individual or organization's attitude is typically described as their dominant disposition, outlook or perspective regarding diversity issues and topics. Developing attitudinal skills requires an empathetic and positive mindset you and your organization must cultivate, way beyond a tolerant mindset towards diversity. It involves curiosity about yourself and the diverse people you communicate and interact with regularly.

Your personal journey begins with *acknowledging* and *correcting* your identified Diversity BAPS to explore diversity further. Our Diversity BAPS (Biases, Assumptions, Prejudices and Stereotypes) are expressed both non-verbally and verbally while communicating and interacting with diverse people. As you embark on your diversity journey or quest, you will experience a myriad of emotions, thoughts and reactions. You also might experience an internal struggle between your heart and your head. Do not worry—this is all a part of embracing change and the growth and development process. I wish you good success on your journey to becoming diversity competent!

Attitudinal Skill #1
Begin a Diversity Journey and Conduct a Diversity Quest

The Diversity Journey

The journey to discover more about diversity is typically a passive route toward learning about individual and cultural differences. Most often, this discovery is unplanned and although you may not be looking for anything in particular, you *will* discover many interesting things about yourself and diverse people along the way.

Two important aspects of a diversity journey are: (1) increased self-awareness and (2) awareness of diverse people. Remember...*diversity awareness is learning what makes us comfortable or uncomfortable, inclusive or exclusive, cooperative or uncooperative when communicating and interacting with diverse people.* The foundation of a diversity journey or quest is establishing the goal of helping us to be more comfortable with diversity issues and diverse people. There are many examples of diversity issues that lead people to diversity discomfort. Some examples include, but are not limited to:

- Certain religious beliefs or nationalities that give rise to unease.

- Gender-related diversity discomforts.

- Heterosexual individuals in the presence of transgender colleagues, customers or students.

These types of diversity discomforts occur because many of us have been indoctrinated with religious and societal teachings that teach us what is acceptable and unacceptable, right and wrong, holy and unholy. When diversity discomfort is present, a diversity journey is critical in helping you make progress in your personal and professional life. A diversity journey is also important so you can learn to communicate and work with diverse individuals more effectively and with a higher level of comfort and confidence.

Various life, school and work events and encounters may fuel a diversity journey. For example, you might have a diversity collision in business with a diverse customer. As a result of this experience, you might develop a desire to explore how getting better acquainted with diversity might affect the way you do business. Many individuals within organizations begin a diversity journey in response to a difficult dialogue, an inappropriate comment, an offensive behavior or negative diversity encounter. As a result, the organization may be at a legal risk and on the verge of an employee or a group of employees pursuing a lawsuit. The downside of learning about diversity in this manner is that the journey becomes forced and mandated, and all that is learned in the process is happenstance and reactive. Anger, irritation and resentment are just a few emotions that describe how individuals may feel when they are forced and mandated to learn more about diversity or cultural sensitivity as a result of diversity-related conflict and tension.

Let us explore an example of beginning a diversity journey.

Please Help Me Understand You (The Diversity Journey)!

The Situation:
Love Towne, Minnesota has seen a massive upsurge in Somali and Mexican immigrants, which is changing the cultural composition of the town. There is a good chance the residents never thought much about the influence of the Somali and Mexican culture until both ethnic groups began to regularly attend church service on Sunday.

The Question:
Do you think the residents of Love Towne, Minnesota were welcoming or unwelcoming, inclusive or exclusive, friendly or unfriendly, comfortable or uncomfortable when communicating and interacting with the Somalis and Mexicans?

The Result:

As a result of the reaction to their presence, the Somali and Mexican people of Love Towne began a diversity journey. Their journey began by attending the weekly church services and beginning the process of communicating and interacting with the pre-existing residents of Love Towne, Minnesota and the members of the church. Additionally, the church member's diversity journey began with arranging "meet and greets" with the Somalis and Mexicans to find out more about their cultural practices. Both groups agreed that an excellent way to increase communication and cooperation while decreasing diversity anxiety and discomfort would be a church dinner during which the congregation could learn more about each other's cultures and ways of life.

As seen in the previous example, people may initiate a diversity journey because they desire to work, learn and live in a stress-free environment. This proactive approach is critical to reducing and preventing diversity conflicts before they arise. Hosting diversity-related workshops or bringing someone in who can help your community, team or organization on their diversity journey is a proactive way to learn more about diversity in a non-threatening way. If individuals and organizations truly want to be diversity competent, they need to invest time, money, energy and resources to accomplish their diversity goals.

Unfortunately, I am often called in to rectify diversity conflicts after the damage is done because organizations have decided to put their diversity concerns and issues on the backburner. Believe me, these kinds of workshops and seminars are not my favorite, but I rise to the occasion every single time. I often tell audiences and organizations that when it comes to learning about diversity, you either pay *now* or you pay *later*, but you will eventually *pay*. Paying upfront is proactive and paying later is reactive, but you always pay regarding diversity-related issues.

The Diversity Quest

So what is the difference between a diversity journey and a diversity quest? The key difference is that a diversity quest is far more intentional. You conduct a diversity quest hoping that your level of discomfort will decrease and strategic goals are made to reduce your diversity discomfort. However, with a diversity journey, you can undertake an organized exploration with the understanding that not all of your educational goals will be predetermined. You can improve your communication skills through either a diversity journey or a diversity quest. A diversity quest is the ultimate exploration you should strive for if you *truly* want to confidently communicate and interact with diverse people.

A diversity quest is much more aggressive, proactive, intentional and purposeful than a diversity journey. When choosing to conduct a diversity quest, the choice to *explore* diversity proactively requires systematic investigation. It is a more deliberate venture. Exploration is usually prodded by an inner desire and will to thoroughly investigate the various diversity issues we wish to examine and learn more about. Questions we may ask ourselves while preparing to conduct a diversity quest include the following.

Diversity Quest Preparation Questions

- Do I even want diversity to be a part of my personal and professional life? If so, which dimensions of diversity do I want to include in my personal and professional life?

- How much diversity am I willing to allow into my personal and professional life (You may feel as though diversity is important in your professional life but find yourself unwilling to allow it into your personal life)?

- What diversity issues or topics do I want to explore?

- What are my areas of diversity incompetence?

- What dimensions of diversity do I need to focus on today, tomorrow and in the future (This involves prioritizing your diversity needs and desires, so your comfort level, with regard to diversity, is maximized as quickly as possible)?

- Who can constructively help me on my diversity quest (Perhaps you will choose to take a class, attend a diversity workshop, purchase diversity movies and documentaries, visit a different type of church or house of faith and worship, have a conversation with a close friend whose diversity competence you trust or read a book that will help you understand diversity)?

- When will I commit and dedicate myself to becoming diversity competent? Are you really going to wait for a diversity crisis to strike or are you prepared to competently and effectively handle a diversity crisis?

- What benefits will there be for me in starting my diversity quest? How much easier will my life be when my confidence around diversity is enhanced by the journey or quest I choose to take?

For schools and organizations, the need to conduct a diversity quest will likely be motivated by diversity issues within the organization and your desire to create a diversity-friendly, inclusive and welcoming environment. If diversity issues are a source of conflict and tension among your leadership, employees and students, then a diversity quest demands immediate attention. I encourage all individuals and organizations to research their opportunities for conducting a diversity quest.

Exploring Diversity: Jermaine's Diversity Quest

Now that I have distinguished between a diversity journey and a diversity quest, I would like to illustrate the process of conducting a diversity quest based on a personal experience. Years ago, I set out on my own diversity quest to discover and learn more about GLBT issues (Gay, Lesbian, Bisexual and Transgender) and sexual orientation diversity in general.

My original beliefs and perceptions of GLBT issues and sexual orientation diversity were developed during my adolescent years through social conditioning. One hundred percent of what I heard about members of the GLBT community growing up was grossly negative, meaning I had no positive information to glean from. I had heard many negative comments from certain family members growing up regarding the GLBT community. Five statements that played a huge role in shaping my beliefs and perceptions and eventually leading to the construction of my Diversity BAPS towards the GLBT community included:

(1) "God made Adam and Eve, not Adam and Steve."

(2) "All gays should be put on one planet, shot and killed."

(3) "All gays are going to Hell."

(4) "Gays are very promiscuous, and they are the reason we have AIDS."

(5) "Do not allow gay men around your young children, especially your boys."

As a result of these destructive messages, I proactively decided to aggressively pursue new knowledge regarding members of the GLBT community. I began my diversity quest by asking questions, renting educational videotapes, attending seminars and workshops and reading books. Also, I accepted an invitation from a student in my public speaking course to attend a GLBT (Gay, Lesbian, Bisexual and Transgender) meeting held on my college campus. Attending our school's GLBT student meeting allowed me to learn more about a community with which I was radically ignorant of. By deliberatively educating myself, I was beginning the process of eliminating and eradicating my GLBT diversity ignorance. I was moving from diversity incompetence to diversity competence.

A Deeper Look at My Diversity Quest: The GLBT Community

Jenny, a student in my public speaking class at the time, asked if I would mentor her efforts in becoming a professional speaker. After agreeing to her proposal of being her mentor, she confided in me by telling me she was a member of the GLBT community. She continued to ask whether I would be willing to attend a GLBT meeting with her. Upon her request, I immediately thought of the quote, "When the student is ready, the teacher shall appear." Although she did not know it, I had recently begun my diversity quest and I found her invitation most intriguing. Jenny's invitation to our college's GLBT student meeting was a prime opportunity for me to further my diversity education and quest.

Instead of avoiding her, I chose to face Jenny and took her proposal as an opportunity to learn and challenge my Diversity BAPS. I viewed Jenny as one of my students and not as Jenny my *GLBT* student. I could have stopped seeing Jenny as a person. Instead, I applied my newly acquired diversity knowledge and chose to look at Jenny as an individual. Jenny's 'diversity' was about to challenge my thinking and expand my horizon.

Although I accepted Jenny's proposal to attend the meeting, I shared my concerns with her by saying, "I want to attend; however, I have a few concerns and questions like: Can I sit in the front of the class, and do

I have permission to be ignorant?" I explained, "I'm very uneducated regarding GLBT issues and sexual orientation diversity." I continued, "I have specific questions regarding the differences between transvestites, transsexual and transgender individuals. I also have questions about cross-dressing. These are issues I know nothing about. As a college professor, I want to be knowledgeable regarding the diversity present in my classroom. I want to know what I don't know about the GLBT community and sexual orientation."

Jenny laughed and responded, "Ask all you want, Professor Davis!"

I recognized and acknowledged that I held Diversity BAPS (Biases, Assumptions, Prejudices and Stereotypes) against members of the GLBT community, and those negative beliefs were affecting how I was communicating and interacting with members of the GLBT community. I decided to confront my diversity discomfort, fear and uneasiness. I did not know what would become of my diversity quest, but I was sure that I did not want my beliefs to cause me to treat other diverse human beings *unfairly.* Conducting a diversity quest steered me in the right direction to work on my Diversity BAPS. As James Baldwin, Civil Rights activist and author once wrote, "You can't fix what you will not face."

Attitudinal Skill #2
Conduct a FEELS Analysis

Ask yourself, "What Difference Does the *Difference* Make?"

All behaviors begin with a basic attitude toward a given diversity issue. To possess attitudinal proficiency regarding diversity implies having the ability to communicate appropriately and effectively across differences. It also means *to possess a fair and favorable mindset when exploring and looking at diversity issues* by being able to see the positive and beneficial aspects of diversity. For example, in some situations, having a diverse workforce and a diverse group of students means ideas generate from many different perspectives. This can greatly increase the chances for finding varied and unique solutions for the organization or school. Additionally, these different viewpoints can be the driving factor behind positive changes in schools and organizations.

Effective exploration of your attitudes regarding diversity involves understanding your Diversity BAPS and with the question: **What difference does the *difference* make?** In other words, what personal challenges or problems do you have with an individual's unique differences? Do you resist diversity because there are some *differences* too foreign for you to grasp and understand? Are you too ethnocentric to embrace the *differences* of others? Are you resentful of having to learn about others' *differences* in the workplace or school? What do you despise most about others' *differences*?

To assist you in the process of answering these questions, I advocate conducting a FEELS Analysis (next page) especially when emotions and personal preferences are getting in the way of an objective assessment of a diversity issue, situation or encounter. The FEELS are the concerns every organization has for the need and right to defend and cultivate an atmosphere of equality and fairness. The FEELS Analysis includes: *Financial* well-being, *Efficiency* of the employees and organization, *Effectiveness* of the employees and organization, the need to operate *Legally* (by protecting the organization's legal well-being) and the *Safety* of the workers (including leaders) of the organization as a whole.

Organizations, especially, will benefit from practicing the FEELS Analysis when personal opinions and preferences regarding diversity issues interfere with workplace equality and fairness. For example, you may find yourself working with someone who is passionately married to their beliefs regarding a diversity issue, so they immediately dismiss or disregard alternative ideas and perspectives. When you consciously choose to conduct a FEELS Analysis, you force yourself and your organization to maintain fairness and equality. Diversity and workplace conflict can be resolved once you conduct an effective FEELS Analysis to discover what the *difference* you or your organization is struggling with.

The five questions (next page) of the FEELS Analysis are designed to help individuals and organizations assess their top priorities regarding diversity. The

FEELS Analysis is multidimensional. It does have a subjective, emotional and visceral quality to it, and it is a rational and logical procedure. Conducting a FEELS Analysis can ensure fair hiring, fair employment practices, equitable promotions and professional termination procedures. This process is designed to stop and eliminate workplace inequalities as well as social injustices.

When the *difference* impacts the organization's FEELS, it may not necessarily be an act of discrimination. It is important to apply the FEELS Analysis when you cannot differentiate between your personal preferences, your Diversity BAPS or whether you have a legitimate concern regarding organizational policies, practices and procedures.

The Five FEELS Analysis Questions

Financial (Monetary Matters): Does the diverse person impact the organization negatively from a financial standpoint? Why or why not? If possible, list that individual's *differences* that may interfere with your organization achieving its financial goal (Please answer from a rational perspective rather than an emotional perspective).

Effectiveness (Achieving Desired Results): Does the diversity this person brings to the organization interfere with the organization's productivity? Are there any diversity-related issues that may interfere with workplace effectiveness?

Efficiency (Task Completion in a Timely Manner): Does the diversity this person brings to the organization interfere with her or his ability to get goals completed in a timely manner? Are there any diversity-related issues that may interfere with organizational goals being completed in a timely manner?

Legally (Legal and Policy Violations): Does the diversity this person brings to the organization violate any company policies, practices or procedures for conducting ethical business?

Safety (Health and Physical Protection): Are there any aspects of the person's unique diversity that violate any company safety regulations or job performance requirements?

This attitudinal skill is a great tool to help you and your organization assess situations that involve diversity. Let us explore and examine how this attitudinal skill can benefit you in the workplace, by putting the following example through the FEELS Analysis.

Using the FEELS Analysis

Scenario: Octavia is responsible for hiring an employee for a construction crew, and she finds herself feeling negatively toward a qualified job candidate who has dreadlocks. Now, answer the question: What difference does the *difference* make?

Financial: Does this potential employee having dreadlocks impact the organization financially? Will the company lose money as a result of the employee having dreadlocks?

Effectiveness: Will the potential employee's dreadlocks interfere with the team or organization's productivity? Will dreadlocks prevent the team from accomplishing their goals?

Efficiency: Will the potential employee's dreadlocks interfere with the tasks being completed in a timely manner?

Legally: Does the potential employee's dreadlocks violate any of the company's policies, practices or procedures, and keep the company from operating ethically?

Safety: Does the potential employee's dreadlocks violate any of the company's safety rules and regulations?

In the previous example, the manager tasked with hiring could secretly harbor Diversity BAPS or fears related to having someone with dreadlocks work for her team or organization. She might be suspicious that the person with dreadlocks has a negative attitude toward authority and because of that perception; she might see the potential employee as ineffective and could potentially cost the organization money. The manager may simply think dreadlocks are an ugly and disgusting hairstyle. She might simply fear that the employee in question is going to be lazy or have a bad attitude. In this example, she is clearly jumping to conclusions based on her perception of dreadlocks.

The fact is, if you see no financial, efficiency, effectiveness, legal or safety concerns or issues, you may be dealing with a diversity issue that is not worth acting on. If hairstyle is a diversity concern or issue for you, examining your Diversity BAPS will be key to preventing discrimination in your hiring process.

The FEELS Analysis is a great and effective tool to use when hiring potential employees. If you are responsible for recruiting and hiring diverse talent for your organization or you are in a leadership position to promote diverse individuals, then conducting a FEELS Analysis should become second nature to you. An organization that does not deliberately consider diversity and diversity issues during their hiring or termination process may face costly and negative legal consequences later on.

It is important when working with the FEELS Analysis, and with diversity in general, to remember that each individual case is unique. It is impossible to generalize from one situation to the next. The philosophy and practice of diversity competence is asking that you observe yourself and apply the questions in the FEELS Analysis regularly.

Attitudinal Skill #3
Assess Your Diversity Attitudes:
What is Your Diversity Attitude (DA)?

Diversity Attitude (DA) is an individual's or organization's dominant disposition, outlook or perspective regarding diversity issues and topics. Your DA is your overall diversity mindset. Your diversity attitude (DA) as an individual or organization will determine if you are a diversity optimist or a diversity pessimist. It is a reflection of whether you view diversity issues and topics as beneficial or as liabilities. Your DA determines if you resolve workplace diversity conflict and tension constructively or destructively. All diversity attitudes are created and cultivated internally and most often expressed externally through non-verbal communication channels. Colleagues, employees, students and customers can detect an individual's and an organization's diversity attitudes by observing their non-verbal cues and behaviors.

The DA of an organization has a profound effect on what gets done or what does not get done in situations where diversity plays a role. Sometimes our diversity attitude can manifest subtly by allowing it to never be spoken of or directly addressed within the organization. A negative diversity attitude can result in offensive comments, inappropriate behaviors and unprofessional body language, which can contribute, to poor workplace communication and a toxic work environment. Do you perceive diversity as positive or negative, good or bad, helpful or hurtful?

There are three types of diversity attitudes that affect an individual's and an organization's actions or inactions when diversity-related issues and topics arise. The three diversity attitudes are: *apathy*, *sympathy* and *empathy*. Consider each kind of diversity attitude as you read the following paragraphs.

Assess You and Your Organization's Diversity Attitude (DA)

Have you ever thought about how you really feel about the topic of diversity? Can you clearly articulate in one sentence your diversity philosophy, including whether you are *for* or *against* diversity? Are you diversity-friendly, welcoming and inviting as an individual or organization? If you are experiencing diversity hostility, ambiguity, ambivalence or uncertainty as an individual or organization, then brainstorm some ideas while answering the following questions:

• Do you view diversity as *harmful* or *helpful*?

• Do you perceive diversity as *positive* or *negative*?

• How is diversity *constructive* or *destructive* for an organization?

• Are you a diversity *critic* and *cynic* or a diversity *cheerleader* and *champion*?

• What is your *real* attitude toward diversity?

Attitudes of *apathy*, *sympathy* or *empathy* motivate our feelings toward diversity. Apathetic individuals "**go through the motions**" during diversity training and study and they *really* do not care about diversity. Sympathetic individuals may encourage an accepting atmosphere, but they do not tend to do anything to cause real change in an organization. They get involved when the risks are really low, and they allow their words to speak louder than their actions. This is the reverse of what most individuals were told by their parents or guardians when they were younger, "Actions speak louder than words." In contrast to the previous two attitudes, empathetic individuals attempt to put themselves in the shoes of diverse people to understand them. Empathetic individuals are often motivated through their ability to comprehend another person's circumstance or point of view. They can transfer empathy into personal action by hiring and working effectively with a wide range of diverse people.

To check where your organization stands on the issue of diversity, consider your diversity experiences and encounters, and respectfully and professionally ask those around you about theirs. However, you have to be careful; some individuals may be apprehensive about telling you the truth regarding controversial, difficult and highly sensitive diversity-related issues. You will have to build personal and professional trust before others will take the risk and make themselves vulnerable. When trust is built and established, then you can engage in honest communication and open dialogue regarding diversity-related issues.

Now, ask yourself, which attitude best describes you and your organization?

Do You or Your Organization Possess an Apathetic Diversity Attitude (DA)?

Apathy in Greek means, "**Without feeling**." Other descriptions of individuals and organizations that possess a diversity attitude (DA) of apathy are described as expressing their dominant outlook on diversity issues, topics and diverse people by using phrases and questions such as:

- "I don't care about diverse people."

- "I don't care about diversity issues and topics."

- "Why are we making a big deal over diversity issues and topics?"

- "Diversity issues and topics don't matter to me personally or professionally."

- "Diversity issues and topics are a waste of my time."

- "Why are we wasting the organization's time, money and resources on diversity efforts, issues and initiatives?"

Remember, those with a DA of apathy are without feelings and emotions concerning diversity-related issues. These individuals and organizations are annoyed, irritated and are often frustrated with diversity-related issues and topics. Those with a DA of apathy are responsible for killing diversity-related legislation and for sabotaging diversity efforts and initiatives within schools and organizations. With a DA of apathy, the more power and control an individual possesses by her or his position in an organization, the more damage and destruction she or he can do to delay and destroy diversity-related causes, legislations, efforts and initiatives. Diversity apathy is one of the main reasons why most diversity efforts are stalled or completely eliminated in life, school and work.

You may be asking yourself why someone would possess such a destructive attitude and have such negative feelings regarding diversity-related issues and topics and diverse people. Honestly, there are too many reasons to explain in this book why an individual might be fostering and harboring these kinds of feelings. However, the individuals and organizations that engage in diversity-unfriendly behaviors are those who do not see the benefits of diversity inclusion and exploring the differences of others.

It is not uncommon for individuals who have a DA of apathy to have the upper hand in life, school and work. This is due to what I call the 3 Ps: (1) Power, (2) Privilege and (3) Prestige. In some cases, they are functioning within a sphere of only helping their family members and friends. Outsiders call this type of behavior nepotism. But to insiders of this group, it is considered keeping the faith amongst one's cohorts and cronies. Finally, individuals with a DA of apathy are operating out of diversity denial; they gravitate toward what they like and avoid what they dislike. They are indifferent toward diverse people and neutral toward diversity because they already possess a certain power, privilege and prestige in the world. As stated by Holocaust survivor Elie Wiesel, "The opposite of love is not hate, it is indifference. The opposite of life is not death, it is indifference to life."

Professor, author and editor, Dr. Julie Thompson says, "I have not met any black folks, Latino folks, Asian folks, Native [American] folks, gay folks or folks with disabilities who did not care about diversity issues. However, I have met a lot of white folks who are apathetical, didn't care, and don't care about diversity. And, I'm white." Does being white prevent individuals from caring about diversity? Absolutely not! Why does it seem as if oppressed groups in our society often take up diversity issues? Dr. Martin Luther King, Jr. once stated, "Why is it always the oppressed that need to teach the oppressor?"

Do You or Your Organization Possess a Sympathetic Diversity Attitude (DA)?

Sympathy in Greek means, "**Affected by like feelings**." Individuals and organizations that possess a DA of sympathy are those who feel a sense of care, concern and compassion for another's diversity challenge or situation, especially in an unfortunate diversity situation. Having a DA of sympathy best describes those who are sensitive toward and feel emotional about diversity-related issues. These individuals are usually saddened and affected by unfortunate events experienced by friends and colleagues or by stories they see on the news or read in newspapers. While feelings of sympathy are meaningful because they communicate thoughtfulness, care and concern, these *emotions without action* are not enough to make a difference in everyday life. Change requires action. Those with a DA of sympathy may *feel* for you, but they will not take *action* for you.

For example, individuals with a DA of sympathy will describe themselves as non-racist, non-sexist or non-homophobic, which means they do not personally participate in discriminatory activities or treat diverse people unfairly because of their diversity. However, this self-description does not guarantee they will advocate for the rights and fair treatment of diverse communities, women and members of the GLBT community.

An example of having a DA of sympathy would be feeling sorry for or becoming very emotional for the person who is visually impaired, the person in a wheelchair or the person with cerebral palsy who walks with a cane or crutches. A person who has a DA of sympathy will exhibit feelings and emotions of care, concern and compassion for the person with the disability. However, feeling sad for a person with a disability does not improve the overall circumstance for that person. A person with a DA of sympathy must be extremely careful that she or he does not pity individuals with disabilities and treat them as less than or incompetent while communicating and interacting with them.

I Have More Abilities than Disabilities

At a diversity workshop I was conducting, a participant named Mona shared a story of how she's often disregarded, overlooked and made to feel *invisible* because of her physical disability. Mona, who navigates life from a wheelchair, stated, "I'm 23 years old and when I'm out at a restaurant with my parents, servers often ask my parents what I would like to eat, and I interrupt them by informing the server that I am capable of ordering my own food." Mona said servers typically stand there frozen because they realize they have just stereotyped her as a person with a disability who cannot do anything for herself. She told the audience how people talk down to her as if she's incompetent and unintelligent. I will never ever forget the powerful statement Mona made when she concluded her story by stating, "Just because my body may not be working the way I want it to, does not mean my mind is not working. People often think just because your body is not working, your mind must not be working as well." She then proceeded on as she spoke with power and conviction, "We are all one accident away from being disabled…one accident away, everyone…just one accident."

Many individuals with disabilities like Mona define themselves according to their abilities rather than their disability or limitation. The philosophy and practice of diversity competence teaches us to appreciate individuals for their abilities and capabilities and not focus on their disabilities and limitations.

Do You or Your Organization Possess an Empathetic Diversity Attitude (DA)?

Empathy in Greek means, "**Passion**." Historically, the Greeks referred to their passion as their "pathos" which means having "**feelings and emotions.**" *Empathy is the ability to intentionally place oneself into another person's experience,*

situation or shoes. An empathetic person deliberatively projects herself or himself into the worldview and perspective of diverse people. The ultimate goal of empathy is to fully understand, identify with and connect with the person you are communicating and interacting with. This can be achieved by adhering to the wisdom of the Native American proverb, "Oh, Great Spirit, let me not criticize another until I have walked a mile in [her or] his moccasins."

Those with a DA of empathy will describe themselves as anti-racist, anti-sexist or anti-homophobic, signifying a more active, assertive and proactive stance regarding social injustice and workplace inequality. When offensive comments and inappropriate behaviors occur in the workplace or school setting, individuals with a DA of empathy will take deliberate action to stop the offensive comments and inappropriate behaviors. Those with a DA of empathy will take action because they have cultivated an *anti*-paradigm toward injustice and inequality. *'Anti'*-ism motivates, stimulates and compels individuals to take action or do the right thing in the face of injustice and inequality.

Individuals and organizations possessing a DA of empathy are those that have a strong desire and motivation to ensure ALL people and dimensions of diversity are celebrated, embraced, honored, respected and valued. These are the individuals within organizations and society who demand and expect that we create friendly, inclusive, welcoming and culturally sensitive communities, schools and organizations. Those with a DA of empathy are adamant about doing the right thing ALL the time. They are diversity change agents because they fight for justice, equality, fairness and freedom of ALL human beings. You may be asking yourself, "Why do people with a DA of empathy have so much emotion, feeling and passion around diversity issues and topics?" It is because they practice the attitudinal skill of empathy, putting themselves in the shoes of diverse people before judging them.

If *all* people were motivated by empathy, the Native Americans would never have been persecuted and driven off their homeland, no slavery would have occurred in America, women would have never been denied the right to vote and the Holocaust would never have happened. Neither would we know the evil works of leaders such as Adolph Hitler, Joseph Stalin, Saddam Hussein, Pol Pot, Bento Mussolini, Idi Amin and many others. What would our world be like if everyone were passionate about human rights, civil rights, social justice and human equality?

Here is an example of how I exhibited a DA of empathy to evoke change and stop violence.

A DA of Empathy on University Avenue

Two years ago, I was taking my cousin Jennifer, who was visiting me, to the Greyhound bus station in Saint Paul, Minnesota, for her trip back to Chicago. As we were driving, I witnessed a disturbing act at the intersection of University Avenue and Rice Street. There in broad daylight a man was assaulting a woman, which I assumed was his wife or girlfriend. He was yelling and screaming profanities, grabbing her wrists and punching the woman in her face. She tried her best to get away, but could not because he was faster, stronger and more aggressive.

Feelings of sympathy would have caused me to say to myself, Thank God, I'm personally not a domestic violent person, and I sure do feel sorry for her situation because I hate to see women in that kind of situation. When possessing feelings of apathy, I may have thought: this matter does not concern me because it is not one of the females I care about or personally know like my mother, grandmother, sister, aunt, cousin or niece. Or I could have thought to myself, "Maybe she's getting what she deserves."

Due to the fact that I am *anti*-domestic violence and *anti*-abusive relationships, I was compelled to take action. Approaching the situation with wisdom, I laid into my horn aggressively, using the loud noise to gain the abusive man's attention. It worked too! The more I honked, the less he hit the woman. Next, I called 911 from my cell phone and reported the incident. I rolled down my window and yelled at him, which created an even greater distraction. He then redirected his anger at me. Ranting and cursing, "Mind your own damn business, etc!" But, my plan worked because the more I distracted him, the less he hit the woman. My *anti*-attitude toward this disgusting act of violence energized me to get up off my butt and take action. This was *definitely* an act of empathy.

Attitudinal Skill #4
Train Yourself to Mentally See Diverse
People as Unique Individuals

The practice of classifying similar dimensions of diversity is the same as stereotyping. This is because the individual's unique characteristics and qualities are disregarded, and they are classified *only* according to their cultural or group membership. This is something that most people are accustomed to doing whether they are aware of it or not. You can condition and train your mind to habitually see people as unique individuals. In order to do this, you have to *intentionally* remind yourself every time you find yourself communicating and interacting with a diverse person to see that person as a unique individual. Keep in mind (regardless of the person's primary dimensions of diversity), that each individual possesses unique characteristics and qualities that make them uniquely different. Consider the following example: There are almost one hundred and fifty million women in the United States of America. If I am going to be effective at communicating and interacting with women, it is mandatory that I do not stereotype ALL women as the same. I can only communicate and interact effectively with a woman when I see and treat her as a unique individual. For example, if I have a bad experience with one female colleague, it is important that I do not begin to treat every other female I meet like the female colleague I had a conflict with.

A habit is an ingrained behavior that has been learned and practiced over a long period of time. Human beings can change their thinking patterns over time by adopting and adapting new thinking habits and practices. For example, after September 11, 2001, many Americans looked at individuals from the Middle East as potential terrorists (I was guilty of this as well). I was trained and conditioned by the American news media to see women and men from Middle Eastern countries as potential terrorists. When I would fly to speaking engagements and see Middle Eastern women or men on the airplane, I had to train myself to see each person as a unique human being. I found myself repeating, "Jermaine, all human beings have unique characteristics and qualities and those characteristics and qualities must be regarded first *before* making assumptions and judgments."

Seeing people as unique individuals requires mental practice and *more* mental practice. One-on-one encounters create wonderful opportunities to get to know diverse people, both personally and professionally. Overcoming your Diversity BAPS requires challenging and refuting the negative perceptions you hold of diverse people. It involves the cognitive practice of giving individuals a clean slate from the moment you meet them. I call this the Clean Slate Theory. *The Clean Slate Theory teaches that human beings are to be seen and treated as credible, innocent, upstanding and just until they have been encountered and experienced otherwise.* If we avoid seeing diverse people as unique individuals, we will begin to view and treat individuals based on the positive and negative experiences we had with the last person who reminds us of them. Whether you see these people as favorable or unfavorable, both perceptions are limiting and dangerous.

Here are two examples of individuals who are not practicing the Clean Slate Theory:

- Mary has had bad experiences having females report to her, so as a result, she automatically dismisses all female candidates.

- Craig loves the two Chileans who work in the global division unit of his shoe apparel business, so he automatically gives his attention to the Chilean job candidate over the Indonesian job candidate.

In both of these examples, Mary and Craig are not practicing the Clean State Theory; they are NOT seeing people as unique individuals. Mary and Craig are connecting these individuals to a specific group and treating them this way based on the Diversity BAPS they hold of those groups.

To be an effective communicator, you have to recognize and accept that there will always be biological, physical and physiological similarities among gender, racial and ethnic groups. However, if you get stuck on looking at an individual's physical traits or identifiable characteristics, you will limit the level of relationship you will have with this person. The goal is to learn to appreciate the unique characteristics and qualities of every individual you meet.

Attitudinal Skill #5
Practice Cognitive Complexity

Cognitive complexity is the ability to mentally look at issues and situations from multiple viewpoints. Practicing cognitive complexity is an attitudinal skill to help individuals and organizations become diversity competent through practicing a form of empathy; it helps people to see diverse issues and situations from another angle and perspective. Looking at issues and situations from only one perspective (your own) makes it difficult to see things differently because your perspective does not include the other person's perspective. When practicing cognitive complexity, you recognize how each of us is comprised of different beliefs, ideas and worldviews. Understanding that we see the world through our own individual perspective and not the perspective of others allows us to realize how biased we can be. It also shows us how much our thoughts can lead to debilitative emotions and irrational decision-making. Jumping to conclusions, over-reacting and stereotyping often happens when individuals and organizations fail to practice cognitive complexity. Cognitive complexity, when practiced effectively, can help individuals observe situations through the eyes of diverse people and perspectives, allowing greater ability to resolve diversity conflict and tension with ease.

Sometimes our deepest empathy comes from practicing *cognitive complexity*. When addressing any diversity conflict or tension, turning the tables and taking on the perspective of diverse people regarding a difficult diversity issue can help you resolve conflict *sooner* rather than *later*. It is important for individuals to know that possessing a DA of empathy does not mean that they have to abandon their own perspective or position.

The University Police and the Students of Color

I was invited to give a presentation on a New York college campus to address diversity conflict and tension primarily between the university police and students of color. The university police at this predominately white school did not carry firearms and the majority of the students of color on the campus were athletes who were African-American and Latino.

These were mostly inner-city urban kids, recruited from the five boroughs of New York: Queens, The Bronx, Brooklyn, Staten Island and Manhattan.

These kids brought along with them their unique diversity, culture and subculture to that upstate New York college campus. And, yes at times they did not always behave as the white students. For example, they congregated in groups, were unified cohesively over campus issues, had different musical tastes and genres and joked around playfully with one another in an expressive manner. The problem was that elements of their culture clashed with the dominant campus culture.

To foster an atmosphere of mutual understanding, I invited both the university police and the students of color to share their perceptions of the existing diversity conflict and tension. Each party had the opportunity to share their perceptions without interruption (deep listening was highly encouraged). Some of the members of the university police stated, "Our sports activities were typically quiet. When we began recruiting and enrolling students of color, these events became boisterous and loud." Fans in attendance were uncomfortable with some of the displays of emotion because they were not used to the celebratory practice of different ethnic groups.

The university police further stated, "The students of color talk loud and play their music loud." The police believed the students were being aggressive in their attitude toward them. They said they sometimes sent negative comments in their direction when they were performing routine patrols in the residence halls and other campus buildings. "I'm just doing my job," one university police officer stated. And, feeling the negative resistance from the students of color, the university police pushed back and became negative as well.

On the other hand, the students of color believed racial profiling was occurring on their campus. They said, "Wherever and whenever we congregate the police immediately show up." They also believed they were treated unfairly, explaining, "When white fraternities and sororities gave loud parties, only a complaint is issued, but students of color are ticketed and fined. The town police are called on us, which makes us believe and feel we are being *unfairly* treated."

I knew from conducting diversity workshops that each party believed their perceptions to be accurate and real. While encouraging the practice of cognitive complexity, I asked that we create a scenario that might enable them to broaden their perception about the situation. I instructed the university police to think as if they were the Latino and African-American students new to the campus environment. I passed out markers and paper and asked them to come up with five to seven emotions they might experience if they were in these students' positions. I asked, "What would go through your mind? How might you feel?" Then I challenged them, "I want you to become a student of color and to think of any challenges or obstacles you might be experiencing as a student of color on a predominantly white college campus."

I asked the students of color to participate in the cognitive complexity exercise as well by taking on the perspective and position of the university police officers. I wanted the students to have firsthand experience in a different role. My goal was to get the students of color to practice empathy with the police officers. By reversing the roles, they were able to recognize the challenges of being a police officer on a college campus and having to ensure safety for ALL students.

There are many individual and organizational benefits to implementing and regularly practicing cognitive complexity. I highly encourage individuals to add this attitudinal skill to their Communication and Diversity Toolbox. With practice, an individual can receive benefits from practicing cognitive complexity, which includes the following:

- Cognitive complexity skills increase your chances of resolving conflict in a healthy and positive manner.

- Cognitive complexity prevents or reduces defensiveness in you and with the people with whom you are communicating and interacting.

It is difficult to resolve diversity conflict and tension when individuals are busy attacking one another and defending their position.

- Cognitive complexity prevents or reduces you and others from over-reacting, jumping to conclusions and passing judgment on others during diversity conflict and tension.

- Cognitive complexity prevents or reduces misunderstandings from occurring or escalating into uncontrollable diversity conflict and tension.

Because of perceptual differences, members of the same organization, school or community may not see eye-to-eye on diversity-related issues. When individuals do not invest the mental and emotional time into understanding why members of their organization believe in the importance of exploring diversity-related issues, more conflict can ensue, eventually leading to diversity-related resentment. To help you and your organization effectively practice cognitive complexity and resolve diversity conflict and tension, consider asking yourself the following questions:

- Why might the other person feel the way they do regarding certain diversity issues? Why are they so passionate about diversity?

- What are they trying to communicate to me regarding their stance on a particular diversity issue or topic?

- How can I communicate to them that I understand their diversity perspective or position?

- What behaviors do they need to see from me to convince them that I understand their diversity perspective or position?

- What expectations do they have of me regarding their diversity issue?

- What is preventing me from understanding their diversity perspective?

- How did they arrive at their conclusion regarding this diversity issue?

When you answer these questions honestly from the perspective of the other person (to the best of your abilities), you communicate respect and open-mindedness. You may not agree with them, but you communicate consideration and a willingness to explore their concerns and issues, which is paramount to resolving any kind of conflict. Remember all human beings want to be *heard* and *understood.*

As with any skill, the more you practice the more you increase you level of proficiency; the more you practice cognitive complexity, the more you will integrate the practice into your everyday life. The ultimate goal of this attitudinal skill is for individuals and organizations to gain a deeper understanding of diverse people.

There are many stories and examples that I have collected over the years to reinforce the attitudinal skill of cognitive complexity. With great conviction, I believe the following example is clearly an "epic story" of cognitive complexity.

In his groundbreaking experiment, John Howard Griffin wanted to improve race relations and racial communication, so he began the process by personally and professionally practicing cognitive complexity. He decided to practice empathy by walking a mile in the shoes of someone else. As a white man in the late 1950s and early 1960s, Mr. Griffin consulted prominent dermatologists to assist him with his diversity quest. How could a white man become a black man? The best method was to darken his skin tone and complexion. This could be done through oral medication followed by exposing his entire body to ultraviolet rays from a sun lamp hours at a time. John Howard Griffin lived for six weeks as a black man and concluded his experiment early because he learned that walking in the shoes of a black man was a difficult experience in the Deep South that he could no longer bear it—mentally, emotionally, physically and spiritually. His experiment reinforced that racism and discrimination were definitely a part of the black man's burden and daily experience.

The Epic Story of Cognitive Complexity and Role Reversal: Black Like Me

Journalist and author John Howard Griffin of the international bestseller *Black Like Me* wrote in his journal (dated October 28, 1959):

"For years the idea had haunted me, and that night it returned more insistently than ever.

If a white man became a Negro in the Deep South, what adjustments would he have to make? What is it like to experience discrimination based on skin color, something over which no one has control?

This speculation was sparked again by a report that lay on my desk in the old barn that served as my office. The report mentioned the rise in suicide tendency among Southern Negroes. This did not mean that they killed themselves, but rather that they had reached a stage where they simply no longer cared whether they lived or died.

How else except by becoming a Negro could a white man hope to learn the truth? Though we lived side by side throughout the South, communication between the two races had simply ceased to exist. Neither really knew what went on with those of the other race. The Southern Negro will not tell the white the truth. He long ago learned that if he speaks a truth unpleasing to the white, the white will make life miserable for him.

The only way I could see to bridge the gap between us was to become a Negro. I decided I would do this. I prepared to walk into a life that appeared suddenly mysterious and frightening. With my decision to become a Negro I realized that I, a specialist in race issues, really knew nothing of the Negro's real problem."

When I first read the book, *Black Like Me*, I thought that John Howard Griffin was a brave and courageous soul. To this day, I have the utmost respect for him for having the mental fortitude, emotional tenacity and physical stamina to embark upon such a controversial and dangerous diversity quest.

Human beings tend to fear what they do not understand. When the emotion of fear is present during the communication process (especially when communicating and interacting with those who are different from us), a healthy interpersonal dialogue never ensues. In this kind of scenario, the emotion of fear would not compel us to get to know and understand the diverse person better, but to avoid them altogether. This is why the emotion of fear is one of the pivotal barriers that prevent individuals and organizations from being diversity competent. What we fear, we resist!

Attitudinal Skill #6
Identify Your Diversity 10-80-10

I want to be up front and honest with you. *Diversity work is hard work, and it requires dedication, determination and discipline to achieve organizational success.* This work can be mentally, emotionally and physically taxing and has led many people to chronic stress and burnout. *Diversity burnout is when an individual loses her or his will and motivation to continue to advocate for diversity fairness, equality, justice and respect for all people.* When diversity advocates lose faith and begin to believe they are helpless and hopeless individuals, then organizations, schools and society in general are doomed and headed for more diversity conflict and tension.

All organizations that succeed at diversity do so because of their Diversity Dream Team. *A Diversity Dream Team is a group of change agents who are committed to helping their organization or school become successful in the area of diversity competence.* Who is on your Diversity Dream Team? Who are the individuals within your organization who *really,* and I mean *really* desire for your organization or school to succeed and become victorious in the area of diversity? Which individuals are determined to help your organization move from diversity discomfort to diversity comfort, from diversity chaos and conflict to diversity communication and cooperation and from diversity incompetence to diversity competence? For diversity initiatives to succeed in any organization or school, the initiatives must be supported and implemented by dedicated, determined and disciplined leaders, employees and students. All organizations need diversity advocates, proponents and supporters at all levels within the organization or school to effect the greatest change.

It is imperative that you, as a diversity advocate, quickly identify within your organization the people that are committed to diversity. You will need to build diversity alliances and bridges with individuals who are dedicated to making your organization or school diversity-friendly, inclusive and welcoming. At times, you will need to depend and rely on your Diversity Dream Team members for mental, emotional and physical support to prevent burnout from occurring. It is important for you to reciprocate and be supportive of them as well. This is why it is so important to quickly identify what I call your Diversity 10-80-10.

These numbers indicate the **top 10%** of organizational members. The **top 10%** of the members in your organization are referred to as, "Diversity Change Agents and Cheerleaders." These are the people who fully understand and share the organization's diversity vision and mission.

The **bottom 10%** of organizational members are referred to as, "Diversity Cynics." These are the people who are overly critical of almost any new idea. These are the people that will never be on board regarding diversity concerns and issues, no matter what you or your organization proposes.

The remaining **middle 80%** of organizational members are referred to as, "Diversity NIMBYs (Not In My Back Yard)." These are the people who will be open-minded enough to explore diversity concerns and issues and diverse people. However, they are not very proactive regarding making change. With help and encouragement, these members can initiate and implement basic changes to improve the climate of the organization.

Let us look at a breakdown of the Diversity 10-80-10.

10%	The Top 10% =
80%	**The Diversity Change Agents**
10%	**and Cheerleaders**

- These are the individuals within organizations and society who possess a DA of empathy regarding diversity-related concerns and issues. The Diversity Change Agents and Cheerleaders are diversity proponents and are proactive when addressing and dealing with diversity conflict and tension.

- **The Top 10%** prefer conflict *prevention* to conflict *intervention*. The Diversity Change Agents and Cheerleaders would rather plan ahead to prevent diversity conflict and tension from occurring rather than avoid diversity conflict and tension *only* to have a major diversity catastrophe occur later.

- **The Top 10%** acknowledge, recognize and respect the fact that other people are different from them. They are also continuously exploring the differences of diverse people. They create diversity-friendly, inclusive and welcoming environments for all people.

- **The Top 10%** see the benefits and importance of diversity and diverse people from a personal, professional and organizational perspective.

- **The Top 10%** do their diversity homework to get to know diverse people better, to improve communication and to avoid stereotyping.

- The diversity work of **The Top 10%** helps the organization move from awareness to action and implementation (they move beyond diversity lip service). They build diversity alliances and bridges with other Diversity Change Agents and Cheerleaders to sustain motivation for this kind of work.

10%	The Middle 80% =
80%	The Diversity NIMBYs
10%	(Not In My Back Yard!)

- **The Middle 80%** are the individuals within organizations and society who possess a DA of sympathy regarding diversity-related concerns and issues. Diversity NIMBYs are indecisive, unclear, uncertain and ambiguous regarding their stance on diversity issues. Some may be more certain of their diversity position and stance, but very apprehensive and reluctant about sharing it with their leaders and colleagues.

- **The Middle 80%** typically will not get involved in diversity-related issues unless the diversity issues, conflict or tension begins to affect them personally or professionally. They do not act until the problem is in their backyard.

- **The Middle 80%** are more *reactive* than *proactive*. The NIMBYs possess an intervention-based mentality rather than a prevention-based mentality.

- The lack of leadership and initiative of **The Middle 80%** are the biggest reasons for organizations and schools remaining diversity incompetent. Some Diversity NIMBYs say, "If it ain't broke, don't fix it," "Those issues don't concern me,"

"That's not my problem—I'm not getting involved," or "I'm just here to work or to obtain my college degree; I'm not here to change the world."

Here is an example regarding **The Middle 80%** (The Diversity NIMBYs).

Not In My Back Yard (NIMBY)!

While attending Elmhurst College, my favorite political science professor, Dr. Andrew Prinz, shared with me the "**I Don't Care**" philosophy of life, otherwise known as the NIMBY (Not In My Back Yard) theory. He wanted me to avoid living a life of apathy. Dr. Prinz wanted me to live a purpose-driven life. He wanted me to be a social change agent no matter what profession I chose. Dr. Prinz informed that, "Most people in life never get involved in social issues because they don't care and the social issue is not in their backyard. However, they will *only* take action when the social issue is in their backyard." He instructed me as a 17-year old, "Jermaine, listen to me, you do not want to live your life on the sidelines. Get involved and get into the game of life and make a difference."

As Dr. Prinz shared this powerful message with me, I began to reflect on a quote by Dr. Martin Luther King, Jr. when he wrote, "I am cognizant of the interrelatedness of all communities and states. *I cannot sit idly by in Atlanta and not be concerned about what happens in Birmingham. Injustice anywhere is a threat to justice everywhere.* We are caught in an escapable network of mutuality, tied in a single garment of destiny. Whatever affects one directly, affects all indirectly. Never again can we afford to live with the narrow, provincial "outside agitator" idea. Anyone who lives in the United States can never be considered an outsider anywhere in this Country."

I must say, I will never ever forget the encouraging words of Dr. Andrew Prinz. To the best of my abilities I have tried to live my life as a *meaningful specific* rather than a *wandering generality*. One sport metaphor says, "Get off the bench and get in the game," I have chosen this philosophy as my course of life. I have chosen not to be a Diversity NIMBY. I want to make a difference in the world and we must all be concerned with everyone's backyard with respect to workplace inequalities and social injustices.

10%	**The Bottom 10% =**
80%	**The Diversity Cynics**
10%	

- **The Bottom 10%** of the individuals within organizations and society who possess a DA of apathy regarding diversity-related concerns and issues are known as Diversity Cynics. Diversity Cynics are negative, pessimistic, faultfinders, whiners and complainers regarding diversity matters in general.

- **The Bottom 10%** often harasses Diversity Change Agents and Cheerleaders in an effort to prevent organizational change and to maintain organizational traditions. Diversity Cynics really attack **The Middle 80%,** the Diversity NIMBYs, because they view them as easy prey to persuade to their side.

- **The Bottom 10%** will passive-aggressively or aggressively sabotage an organization that is trying to improve its diversity efforts by blatantly refusing to honor and implement new diversity initiatives.

The percentages explaining the Diversity 10-80-10 philosophy may seem menial to you; however, these percentages represent how change occurs or does not occur in organizations. All organizational change begins at the top because leaders possess the powers to create change and get things done. It is critical that organizations understand where their leaders stand within the Diversity 10-80-10 philosophy. If your leadership team functions as **The Top 10%,** as Diversity Change Agents and Cheerleaders, the students and employees of your organization will see and experience an organization that is diverse, inclusive and welcoming.

If your leadership team functions as **The Middle 80%**, as Diversity NIMBYs, the students and employees of your organization will see and experience what I call *stop-n-go* success, which is similar to the phenomenon of *stop-n-go* traffic. In other words, due to the indecisive and reactive attitude of Diversity NIMBYs, students and employees become easily frustrated and irritated because they do not feel they are achieving the diversity goals of the organization fast enough. It is difficult for students and employees to sustain motivation regarding diversity issues, when there is very little organizational progress made as a result of *stop-n-go* success. *Stop-n-go* success eventually kills motivation and drive, leaving students and employees feeling personally and professionally stressed and burned out.

If your leadership team functions as, **The Bottom 10%** as Diversity Cynics, the students and employees of your organization will see and experience organizational inequalities and injustices with regards to diversity issues. When leaders are Diversity Cynics, get ready to see your organization's reputation exposed throughout the community and media as a result of discrimination cases being filed. Diversity Cynics create organizations that are diversity-unfriendly, exclusive and unwelcoming. Diversity Cynics do not *value* diversity; they *disregard* diversity.

No matter where you are within an organization, your actions have an effect. You have the ability to make change within your organization and on your college campus. Making change begins with facing the realities of injustice and inequality that exist within your organization. James Baldwin reinforces this idea when he writes, "Not everything that is faced can be changed, but nothing can be changed until it is faced."

Remember that change begins with your motivation to want to correct injustices and inequalities within your organization. No organization or college campus changes until the individuals within those institutions are willing to change. So will you or won't you change? Which best describes your Diversity 10-80-10? Are you a Diversity Change Agent and Cheerleader, a Diversity NIMBY or a Diversity Cynic? **Choose wisely!**

Be the Force for Change: The Law of Inertia

The Law of Inertia is the first law of the 17th century scientist Sir Isaac Newton. As it applies to physics, it states, "An object at rest tends to stay at rest, and an object in motion tends to stay in motion with the same speed and in the same direction unless acted upon by an unbalanced force." In other words, *objects tend to continue doing what they are doing unless acted upon by an outside force.* The Law of Inertia is replicated in the human experience as well, particularly in the realm of diversity issues.

People continue thinking the same thoughts and practicing the same behaviors over and over again unless they are challenged to think or behave differently by an outside force.

Diversity incompetent individuals and organizations will continue to behave and communicate in the same way they have always been behaving and communicating until someone either *inside* the organization or *outside* of the organization challenges them to think and behave *differently.*

To bring diversity into the forefront, it takes a force—sometimes just one person—to stimulate change. Have you ever thought about being that person who prevents Inertia from occurring within your community, house of faith or worship, organization or school? Can you picture yourself helping individuals and organizations move from diversity chaos and conflict to diversity communication and cooperation? How will you stop Inertia from occurring? If you decide to challenge the Inertia of your organization or school, can you help them move from diversity incompetence to diversity competence? ABSOLUTELY!

Organizations can only transition from diversity chaos and conflict to diversity communication and cooperation when they have individuals within the organization challenging the Inertia of the organization; in other words, courageous leaders, students and employees have the power to challenge the organization's inequalities and injustices.

New diversity affects the organization's culture, and at times challenges and stretches the organization's traditional beliefs and values in ways it may have never been challenged and stretched before. This challenging and stretching may annoy, irritate and frustrate many leaders and employees because many of them want to continue doing business and/or things as usual.

It takes the actions of one or a few people to overcome Inertia and to create a change that incorporates diversity into what is happening in society, in the community or in the workplace. Undoing the edict, "We've always done it this way," requires removing our Inertia and stepping up to make the changes that need to be made in order to make our organizations and schools more diversity-friendly, inclusive and welcoming.

Asking yourself questions can help you identify where diversity needs representation. Can you see places in society, in your organization or school, where diversity issues are treated with Inertia? How can you learn to be the one to step up and overcome your Inertia and create change? The results from critically answering and taking action on those important questions is seen in a previous story when Branch Rickey overcame a country filled with Inertia about people of color in major league baseball. It took the diversity courage that he and a few other Change Agents possessed to break through that barrier and mobilize others toward change. Again, it takes diversity courage to challenge "the norm," but all it takes is one person to say that diversity is needed in order to advocate for it. You do not need to be an executive, have a fancy job title or be wealthy to be the one to help individuals and organizations overcome Inertia.

Behavioral Skills

"Jermaine, actions speak louder than words," uttered my mother when she wanted me to focus on paying closer attention to how I was *behaving* rather than on what I was *saying*. Ralph Waldo Emerson affirms my mother's wisdom when he writes, "What you do speaks so loud I cannot hear what you say." I agree with my mother and Mr. Emerson; how we *behave* while communicating and interacting with diverse people is more potent than the actual words we use at times. Diversity competent individuals are concerned with *how* their body language is perceived and received in the communication process. They know that non-verbal communication can be either intentional or unintentional. However, it is the latter of the two that often leads to diversity conflict and communication misunderstandings in life, school and work.

You cannot *not* communicate while interacting with diverse people. Your Diversity BAPS (Biases, Assumptions, Prejudices and Stereotypes) will communicate your true diversity attitude and comfort level as you engage with diverse people. Sometimes, we attempt to conceal and mask our diversity discomfort, only to have it unintentionally leak out during times of stress, frustration and intense emotional moments.

Authors Adler, Proctor and Towne of the interpersonal communication textbook, *Looking Out Looking In,* define **leakage as, "Non-verbal behaviors that reveal information a communicator does not disclose verbally."** Are there messages you attempt to conceal from the diverse people you are communicating and interacting with when you feel uncomfortable with her or his diversity? Communication research reveals that some of the messages that we attempt to hide from those we feel uncomfortable with eventually leaks out during a diversity encounter. During the communication process, people pay more attention to what you *do* rather than what you *say.*

Can People Tell What I Believe and Think by My Body Language?

Can an individual's body language communicate their DA (diversity attitude)? Most definitely! During any communication exchange or encounter, both the communicator and listener attempt to decode each other's words and behaviors to ensure complete understanding. When a communicator's words are questionable and the words they speak do not match her or his body language, the listener will tend to believe what they see in the communicator's body language rather than what they hear. People look to see what your body language is communicating during diversity-related encounters. This is especially true when people of color and white people are engaged in dialogue or when "out" members of the GLBT community interact with heterosexuals.

So what does your body language actually reveal during the communication process? Renowned UCLA Professor of Emeritus of Psychology, Dr. Albert Mehrabian, found in his highly respected non-verbal communication study that **"93% of all messages are communicated non-verbally while only 7% of messages are communicated verbally."** He breaks down the 93% of non-verbal communication into two categories: our 55% and our 38%. Dr. Mehrabian explains that during the communication process, 55% of an individual's message is communicated and understood through their body language (facial expressions, eyes, gestures and posture) and 38% of an individual's message is communicated and understood through the tone of their voice (not their actual words but the emotional tone behind their words).

The philosophy and practice of diversity competence instructs us that effective individuals and organizations are cognizant of their verbal and non-verbal messages while communicating and interacting with diverse people.

Dr Mehrabian's non-verbal communication study is often described and referred to as the 7%-38%-55% Rule.

7%-38%-55% Rule:
Albert Mehrabian's Three Elements of Communication

7% of a message is received and understood by choice of *words*.

38% of a message is received and understood by *tone of voice*.

55% of a message is received and understood by *body language*

Dr. Albert Mehrabian's 7%-38%-55% Rule reveals how individuals, during diversity encounters and interactions, attempt to determine if other individuals and organizations are racist, sexist, homophobic and intolerant of diversity. Right, wrong or indifferent, you must remember that people cannot see what is going on inside of your head and heart, but they will evaluate and assess how they believe you are as a person by the way you treat them. They do this by decoding your 7%-38%-55% during the communication process.

One practical tool to put inside your Communication and Diversity Toolbox is to regularly ask yourself during diversity encounters and interactions:

- What is my **55%** communicating right now?
- What is my **38%** communicating right now?
- What is my **7%** communicating right now?

Leakage: 55%-38%-7%

How do individuals assess whether an environment is diversity-friendly, inclusive and welcoming? First, they determine who *you* are based on *how* you communicate and interact with them. Your diversity competence can be assessed based upon your body language (non-verbals) and the words you use. During uncomfortable diversity encounters, leakage can manifest non-verbally (our 55%), verbally (our 38%) as well as through the actual words we use (our 7%). Consider the following examples of how an individual's leakage manifests in everyday situations when they experience diversity anxiety and discomfort.

Body Language Leakage (your 55%)

"Leakage" in body language can manifest in the following ways:

Body Language Leakage (your 55%)

- Shifting posture.
- Tapping fingers.
- Scratching one's head.
- Twirling and pulling one's hair.
- Periodically touching one's face.
- Clicking one's mechanical pen.
- Appearing extremely tough, stoic and aggressive.
- Possessing a poker face.
- Clenching one's fist.
- Biting and grinding one's teeth.
- Stuttering when one does not typically stutter (mouth movements).
- Breaking and avoiding eye contact.
- Blinking and rapid eye movement.
- Demonstrating inconsistent body language (This is known as incongruency. *Incongruency is a disconnect between what is said and how one behaves.)*

Here are a few examples of leakage when interacting with diverse people that can be displayed in our everyday body language:

- A look of disgust on someone's face when she or he sees a gay couple holding hands as they walk down the street.

- A look of disappointment on someone's face when she or he sees an interracial couple (for example, a white male with a dark-skinned African-American woman).

- A woman or man adopting a defensive posture when a fellow Christian tells her or him that she or he is a proponent or supporter of gay marriage.

- Someone flaring her or his nostrils and widening of her or his eyes when a lesbian states that she is a Muslim.

Verbal Leakage (your 38%)

Verbal leakage is when a person speaks with an emotional tone and pitch that is arrogant, condescending, demeaning, degrading, disrespectful and overall offensive. During uncomfortable diversity encounters, some individuals may unintentionally leak out their diversity attitude by adopting a very matter of fact tone; you may hear in their voice sounds of fear and trembling and sounds of agitation and irritation. These sounds are quite apparent when individual's affinity levels are unfavorable regarding a certain kind of diversity. You may hear sounds of frustration and impatience in an individual's voice when they are communicating with non-native speakers of English and communicators with heavy accents and different dialects.

Word Usage Leakage (your 7%)

The choice of words and phrases we use while communicating and interacting with diverse people reveals our level of diversity awareness and diversity competence. Offensive and inappropriate words and phrases are likely to leak out when a diversity encounter leads to agitation, frustration and high emotions. Your *true* diversity attitude will show during these times. Are you using words that are diversity-friendly, inclusive and welcoming? Are you sensitive toward the diversity of others? Do you use any of the following labels or phrases:

• Fat people	• Oriental people
• Retarded people	• Colored people
• Handicapped people	• We "jewed" them down
• Old people	• We got "gypped"
• Homosexuals	• Faggots and sissies

The philosophy and practice of diversity competence teaches us that competent communicators use inclusive language rather than exclusive language because exclusive language alienates diverse people. Using biased language can destroy your credibility when communicating and interacting with diverse people. In the world of business, your diversity vocabulary can determine whether you gain business or lose business.

These are just a few examples illustrating how our behaviors communicate strong messages and can determine if people perceive you as diversity-friendly or unfriendly. Yes, your behaviors *do* matter! Your behaviors are either deal makers or deal breakers. Your trustworthiness as a person will be determined by the behaviors you display while communicating and interacting with diverse people. Developing appropriate and effective behavioral skills requires individuals to become self-aware of how they come across to others during diversity encounters. What messages are your non-verbals communicating when interacting with diverse people?

The Twin Towers of Subtle Discrimination: Microinequities and Negative Micromessages

According to UCLA Professor of Emeritus of Psychology, Dr. Albert Mehrabian, the communication we disperse verbally and non-verbally when interacting with diverse people is a combination of our 55%, 38% and 7% communication. As stated earlier, we communicate both intentionally and unintentionally; however, the focus of understanding the leakage factor is to become aware of our unintentional communication to prevent diversity blunders and communication mishaps from occurring.

Our Diversity BAPS, if unchecked, can lead to both intentional and unintentional discrimination. One goal of *Be Diversity Competent* is to help individuals and organizations become more aware of their subtle discrimination and negative communication habits, which can be disrespectful, exclusionary and illegal.

Negotiation and Conflict Management Professor Mary Rowe of MIT (Massachusetts Institute of Technology) Sloan School of Management "coined" the term Microineqities in the early 70s. Professor Rowe is responsible for conducting the groundbreaking and original research on the topic of subtle workplace discrimination and its effect on employees' morale, productivity, self-esteem, absenteeism and turnover rates.

So what are Microinequities? ***Microinequities are messages that are small and subtle, conscious and unconscious and non-verbal and verbal, which demean, devalue and exclude others.*** Microinequities are definitely communicated by way of our 55%, 38% and 7% when we communicate and interact with diverse people.

Here are a few scenarios that provide examples of Microinequities:

- An organization wants to attract and recruit more students and employees of color with a recruitment video. However, the organization's in-house production team cast actresses and actors who are not of color for the video. When the casting director is asked, "How can you make a recruitment video targeted towards people of color and *not* have people of color in the video?" The casting director responds, "I didn't even *think* about it."

- There is a sales team of ten that consists of two women and eight men. The sales director is a man as well. Whenever he plans team outings, he most often plans team activities that are sports-related and male-centered. He fails to consider the interests of the women on his team. When asked by one of the women on his team to consider other options or gender-neutral options, he responds, "I *see* you both as one of the *guys*. Come on—we're all a team. You're just *like* one of the *fellas*."

- Annie had taken three courses with one of her favorite college professors. The college professor had a classroom ritual of putting a Quote of the Day on the dry erase board daily. The Quote of the Day was the beginning discussion for the class before he taught on the day's subject matter. After a year and a half of taking courses with the professor, Annie finally musters up enough courage to ask the professor why he never selects quotes from women to use as the Quotes of the Day. The professor responds, "Wow, you're right! I always select male quotes. I need to think about why I consciously and unconsciously select male quotes. Annie, I promise to be more deliberate about being inclusive. Please forgive me."

From that day forward the professor changed his thinking and practices and became more inclusive of the diversity represented in his college classrooms. Annie inspired him so much that he dedicated his college sabbatical for an entire year towards studying women's issues. The professor went on to write two books dedicated to women's issues: *You Don't Have to Sell Out to Stand Out: 50 Professional Women Speak Out and 207 Stand Out Quotes to Help You Succeed in Life, School & Work.*

So what are Micromessages? **Micromessages are positive and negative messages that communicate value or devalue, respect and disrespect and encouragement and discouragement.** Microineqities are communicated through negative Micromessages. Microinequities and Micromessages can determine if employees within an organization, students within an educational institution, residents of a neighborhood or members of a church, mosque, temple or synagogue feel welcome and included. I often tell organizations and schools that are trying to attract, recruit and retain employees and students of color, to evaluate and pay close attention to their Microinequities and Micromessages. Microinequities and Micromessages are paramount factors that can determine if employees and students of color are retained and if they perceive the environment as diversity-friendly, inclusive and welcoming.

On Microinequites and Micromessages, a magazine article written by Brigid Moynahan in *Executive Action* titled, "Diversity in the Workplace...Go Ahead: Sweat the Small Stuff says,"

"Microinequities may be small, but they pose a major issue for

businesses today. Left unchecked, these inequities will accumulate and become a drag on employee productivity, corporate culture, and, ultimately, a company's ability to keep top talent.

These behaviors and messages are quite prevalent today. In fact, most of us have probably (and unwittingly) engaged in some form of exclusionary behavior. Do you tend to "do lunch" with the same people? Or meet with the same group after work? Have you ever rolled your eyes at a co-worker's "off the wall" comments, and then found yourself praising that same idea when offered by someone you trust? Do you share certain information with close colleagues, but delay in telling others at the same level? Do you rely on the same trusted allies to get a tough job done rather than involving a broader, more diverse group to help? Do you golf with colleagues who look and act just like you? Have you ever deliberately left someone off an email distribution?

The subtle (and sometimes not so subtle) behaviors we use to act out our differences are all examples of Microinequities. Individuals might ask questions or say comments such as: "What's the harm in always having lunch with Tom?" or "forgetting" to cc: a co-worker. The harm, of course, is felt by those left out—those who have been treated inequitably."

Professor Mary Rowe of MIT, in her original research, wrote of the mental and emotional effects of Microinequities and Micromessages on employees in the workplace. Her findings are extremely informative and worthy of consideration for anyone that is committed to creating work and school environments where all employees and students can thrive and succeed. Consider a few of Mary Rowe's thoughts on subtle discrimination:

"I believe that subtle discrimination is a major barrier to equal opportunity and can cause serious damage, for the following reasons:

- *Subtle discrimination often leads to more explicit discrimination. Thus, ignoring women is a habit that may lead to overlooking a woman who might be the best-qualified person for a job promotion or underpaying women.*

- *Because the provocation for discrimination [against] one's gender cannot be changed and has nothing to do with one's work, one inevitably feels helpless.*

- *Subtle discrimination takes up the victim's time. Sorting out what is happening and dealing with one's pain and anger takes time. Extra time is also demanded of many women and men to help other women deal with the pain caused by subtle discrimination.*

- *Discrimination prevents people from doing work that is as good as they are capable of doing. If a secretary or graduate student is unreasonably overloaded with menial work from a supervisor, the overloaded person may be prevented from doing the kind of excellent work that prepares her for a promotion. Subtle forms of discrimination can cause much damage before they are recognized.*

- *Discrimination often is perpetuated by more powerful people—most of whom are male—against less powerful people—most of whom are female. Since less powerful people by definition have less influence, it is difficult for them to stand up against discriminators who happen to be their supervisors or advisors."*

Yes, no matter the environment, Microinequities and negative Micromessages are definite deal breakers for diverse people. The awareness and prevention of both will contribute to a healthy and positive environment where employees and students will be more productive, effective and efficient in their work. It is important to understand that anyone can use Micromessages in a positive manner by communicating powerful and uplifting messages to show respect, support and value to all people. In addition to landing positive Micromessages, I would like to coin the phrase Microequities. *Microequities happen when individuals and organizations use small and conscious, non-verbal and verbal messages to communicate value, respect and encouragement toward all people.*

I wish you good success in adding Microequities and positive Micromessages to your Communication and Diversity Toolbox!

Ethnocentrism and Assimilation

While teaching at North Hennepin Community College in Brooklyn Park, Minnesota, I learned a valuable lesson on ethnocentrism and assimilation as outlined in the following story.

When the *Teacher* is Ready, the *Student* will Appear!

I was teaching public speaking, and a foreign exchange student from Africa was asking questions of how to improve as a public speaker for his upcoming persuasive speech. As I analyzed his behaviors through my American filters and lens, I felt disrespected and eventually became annoyed as he repeatedly asked questions with his eyes focused on the floor and his head in a bowed position. As an American, I believed he should have been asking me questions while maintaining direct and respectful eye contact. What's interesting about this story is that I knew better because I had taken non-verbal communication and studied intercultural communication theory in graduate school at the University of Wisconsin-Superior.

I really knew better than to behave in an ethnocentric manner. However, that day I was practicing ethnocentrism and cultural insensitivity. My student from Africa eventually explained to me that in his native country and culture, looking a professor directly in the eye while addressing her or him is a sign of disrespect and is perceived as a challenge to their authority. WOW! What an *Ah-Ha* moment for me! I later explained to him that I understood how his culture had shaped and influenced the way he interacted in the world. I went on to say that American culture and values has shaped and influenced the way I communicate and interact in the world as well.

Of course, I explained to the student that successful public speaking and interpersonal communication within the American culture expects and requires a healthy exchange of eye contact during conversation and dialogue. I encouraged the student to maintain his cultural identity and practices, but to keep in mind that success in life, school and work in America requires cultural adaptation and not assimilation.

Cultural adaptation is the process of adding to, enhancing and expanding one's cultural practices and perceptions to achieve success in one's present environment.

Conversely, *assimilation, which is the opposite of cultural adaptation, is where an individual loses and replaces her or his primary identity to take on the identity of the dominant culture in order to succeed in life, school and work.*

The issue of assimilation versus cultural adaptation is very controversial because many people believe and feel that "you've got to do whatever you've got to do" to succeed in life. However, there are others who believe they want to succeed in all environments, but not at the cost of losing their culture, pride, integrity and identity.

Are You One of Us or Not?

When diverse people work together or live near one another with different cultural backgrounds, one of two things can happen. First, there is a risk of *cultural assimilation*. With assimilation, at least one of the diverse groups must choose to replace who they are, abandon their worldviews and eliminate their cultural practices in order to become accepted by the dominant culture or group. In other words, the philosophy of cultural assimilation typically teaches newcomers to give up who they are in ordered to be accepted by the dominant culture or group. Many people assimilate in life, school and work, so they can fit in and to make life a little easier for themselves.

But what is the cost of cultural assimilation? Clearly, the newcomers lose their sense of identity because they are desperately trying to fit in while seeking acceptance from the dominant culture or group. Employees and students who decide to assimilate often do so with regret. Many traditionalists believe that cultural assimilation is critical for organizational success. In many organizations, cultural assimilation is expected of immigrants, people of color and women. They are asked either explicitly or implicitly to give up their personal ways of being in order to belong to the dominant culture or group.

What is the cost of cultural assimilation to the dominant culture or group? They fail to learn and be influenced by the newcomer's beliefs, perspectives and cultural insights and practices. Diverse perspectives can provide organizations and schools with the competitive advantages they need to survive in today's ever-changing economy. Cultural assimilation completely stifles the beliefs, creativity, traditions and values of the newcomers. Remember—employees and students need to be able to create and innovate to maximize their fullest potential. It becomes difficult to create and innovate when you cannot be yourself because you are too preoccupied with fitting in and seeking acceptance and approval.

The other possibility is *cultural adaptation.* When this occurs, the newcomers learn the norms, traditions and cultural practices of the dominant group, and the dominant group learns of the norms, traditions and cultural practices of the newcomers. When individuals and organizations practice cultural adaptation, ethnocentric attitudes and behaviors are quickly replaced with respect and mutual understanding for one another's cultural practices. The philosophy of cultural adaptation says, "My culture *if* embraced affects and influences your culture. Your culture *if* embraced affects and influences my culture."

Cultural adaptation encourages and increases communication between diverse groups of people. This philosophy teaches that *my* culture must be able to have a presence in the organization, and *your* culture must also be able to have a presence in the organization. The ultimate goal of cultural adaptation is to create a win-win culture where all cultural perspectives and ways of doing things are regarded, respected and valued. I wish you good success as you and your organization practice cultural adaptation to improve the overall climate of your workplace or school.

Behavioral Skill #1
Be Aware of and Self-Monitor Your 55%

Your DA (diversity attitude) plays a huge role in determining the types of body language you display when communicating and interacting with diverse people. In other words, your internal attitudes and beliefs are often conveyed non-verbally through your 55% (facial expressions, eyes, gestures and posture). Meaning, you can only "fake it" for so long before your real emotions and feelings are communicated through your body language. Your 55% will tell others during diversity encounters whether you perceive them as friend or foe, ally or enemy, valued customer or potential shoplifter.

For example, imagine you manage a retail store. Do you experience diversity discomfort when an interracial couple walks into your retail store holding hands? What does your body language communicate to them? The DA you hold regarding this particular diversity encounter can easily be displayed in your body language (your 55%) leaving your customers feeling either welcome or unwelcome. Customers will measure their customer service experience based upon their communication and interaction with you as a service provider. While customers cannot detect your true intentions or read your mind, they will attempt to read and decode your body language (your 55%). Your non-verbal communication can make or break the sale of a big-ticket item they were looking to purchase. So how you *behave* does matter! Ask yourself: what is my 55% saying while communicating and interacting with diverse clients, colleagues or students?

Make Your Non-verbal Communication Congruent with Your Diversity Attitude (DA).

As a communicator, your 55% will often indicate how you are feeling and what you are thinking about regarding diverse people. Do you view a rainbow-colored Mohawk as an artistic expression or appalling? More importantly, what does your 55% communicate as you interact with the person with the rainbow-colored Mohawk?

When I first started my teaching career as a college professor at a predominantly white college, the first day of class was often emotionally nerve-wracking for me. Some students often judged me before they even gave me a chance. Why was I judged? I was a young, black male teaching at a predominantly white institution. The faculty, staff and student population of color was less than one percent. How did I know I was being judged? I was informed by a group of my colleagues that many of the students were from farming towns and communities, which possessed very little or no ethnic diversity. A few of my colleagues eventually revealed to me that a few students had questioned them regarding my competency level once they realized I would be their professor. I recall some occasions where students would abruptly walk out of the classroom when I revealed myself as their professor. I paid close attention to my students' 55% (facial expressions, eyes, gestures and posture) to gauge their DA towards me as a professor of color.

When I think about how I felt during my challenging diversity experience, I was never mad or disappointed at my students' culture shock because I realized that I represented a new experience and new kind of diversity for many of them. I was more hurt and disappointed when the students allowed their Diversity BAPS to interfere with them getting to know me as Jermaine M. Davis the individual rather than Jermaine M. Davis the black man. I was not given a chance to express my individuality and the content of my character as Dr. Martin Luther King, Jr. so passionately spoke of in one of his famous speeches.

Facial expressions, eyes, gestures and posture often express what people may find difficult saying out loud. At times, there can be a big disconnect between an individual's intentions and the impact of their body language on others during the communication process. This disconnect has led to countless communication and diversity misunderstandings. An individual can have the greatest and most sincere intentions in the world, but if their intentions are communicated inappropriately and offensively, her or his intentions will be measured by how people felt after hearing those remarks. The key to using your 55% appropriately and effectively is to self-edit and self-monitor your non-verbal communication regularly.

An Example of Intention vs. Impact
He Didn't Just Say What I Thought He Said, Did He?

A friend invited me to a holiday dinner one year. This family regularly opens up its doors to individuals who may not be able to be with their immediate family during the holidays.

There were a couple of new faces that I saw at the gathering this particular year, and as we sat at the kitchen table making small talk, one gentlemen asked, "So Jermaine, what do you do for a living?" I replied, "I'm a college professor of communication studies." He wanted to know of the various colleges and universities I've taught at over the years. I named two Minnesota schools where I had spent time teaching—Hennepin Technical College and North Hennepin Community College. Both community colleges were located in a northwestern suburb of Minneapolis known as Brooklyn Park. As I named the schools, he stopped and said, "Yeah I'm familiar with both of those colleges—they're located in *Brooklyn Dark*, Minnesota." I paused to capture my thoughts and I replied, "Excuse me I'm sorry, did I misunderstand you?" He replied, "Yeah, they're both located in *Brooklyn Dark* off Brooklyn Boulevard."

At that point, I felt a sense of uneasiness as a black man sitting in a predominantly white setting because he was referring to the changing demographics of Brooklyn Park, Minnesota. Brooklyn Park had become more diverse and yes, the color composition of Brooklyn Park had changed from a predominantly white suburb at one point to more of a mosaic of ethnic groups and cultures over the years.

This example illustrates a classic case of a negative diversity encounter due to impact versus intention. Now let me clarify that I do not believe this gentleman was an evil and racist man. However, his 7% (the actual words he used) revealed his diversity attitude toward how he felt about the changing demographics of Brooklyn Park, Minnesota.

As you practice treating people as individuals, strive to become someone who is a "high self-monitor." *Self-monitoring implies paying close attention to what you say, what you do and how you are saying it.* It may mean asking yourself, "Was I rude?" If you said something that did not feel right after the fact or conversation, then you may have been acting in a rude and disrespectful manner.

One way to self-monitor is to pay close attention to your body position. You may notice that your body position relays a lot of information. Some of the messages are relatively simple, such as trust or the lack thereof. Often if you feel intimidated or easily threatened by another person, you will not stand up to her or him. You will position yourself off to the side instead of standing face-to-face with this person to alleviate potential conflict.

On the other hand, if you are standing in a group and others enter into the group, you usually will turn or open your hips and shift your feet to make eye contact with the new person entering the group. This gesture or some combination of these behaviors creates an inviting atmosphere. Usually, when you are enthusiastic and/or very friendly, then you may apply more of these non-verbal cues at a time. Likewise, there are many ways to close diverse people out. Learn to observe yourself in order to help identify your Diversity BAPS, and then try changing what you are doing if you discover that you are being inconsiderate and exclusionary. Again, assessing your 55% may be as simple as being aware of those you greet and those you do not greet at a meeting. Even simpler, your eye contact (or lack thereof) with diverse people can reflect what you are *not* saying out loud.

How is Your 55% Communicated Non-verbally in Your Interactions with Diverse People?

Remember that you cannot *not* communicate, and the body conveys hundreds of messages throughout the course of an interaction, both intentionally and unintentionally. Diverse people will decode your 55% to determine your diversity attitude, your Diversity BAPS and your diversity-friendliness or unfriendliness. Let us examine four types of non-verbal communication that reveal a great deal about our 55%.

(1) Facial Expressions

When people look at your facial expressions during diversity encounters, what do they see? Are your facial expressions inviting or uninviting, pleasant or unpleasant, opened or closed? In their highly respected and well-known book, *Unmasking the Face,* Paul Ekman and Wallace Friesen conclude that there are six primary emotions that human beings emote when communicating and interacting with one another. These primary emotions include surprise, fear, disgust, anger, happiness and sadness. Remember, diverse people will see your facial expressions before they hear what you say. Your facial expressions create the communication climate even before you utter your first word or first sentence. Your facial expressions can either start a conversation or stop a conversation.

What are you communicating in your facial expressions when communicating and interacting with diverse people? Consider making a list of facial expressions that are diversity-friendly, inclusive and welcoming. Make another list of facial expressions that are diversity-unfriendly, exclusive and unwelcoming.

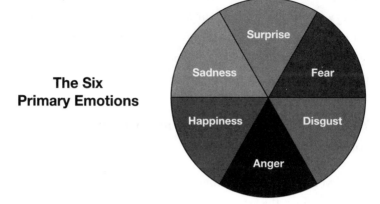

**The Six
Primary Emotions**

(2) Eyes

Your eyes are so powerful that they can communicate whether you are believable or unbelievable. When you maintain appropriate and respectful eye contact with the diverse people you are communicating and interacting with, you increase your believability and credibility factor. When you deliberately make eye contact during a diversity encounter, your actions communicate to the diverse person that you acknowledge and recognize their existence and presence. This, of-course, is a great start for an interpersonal exchange.

The opposite of making eye contact is when a person deliberately avoids making eye contact with diverse people. This is called nonreciprocal eye contact. ***Nonreciprocal eye contact is when one person shows interest in another person by maintaining eye contact and the other person avoids making eye contact or deliberately looks away.*** These kinds of Microinequities and negative Micromessages (which we discussed earlier) communicate powerful diversity messages regarding the atmosphere of an organization. Below are a few examples of nonreciprocal eye contact:

• Jamal, a 19-year-old African-American comes home on his college spring break and brings his new girlfriend, Matayla home to meet his parents. Matayla, who is from Serbia, is happy to meet Jamal's family. She immediately makes eye contact with his mother and father as she enters the family room of the house, but Jamal's parents only greet her verbally without making eye contact.

- A group of eleven white men are all part of a class action lawsuit. They are suing their company for reverse discrimination. The eleven employees believe they were unfairly denied job promotions due to the company's diversity initiative to recruit more women and men of color. Kenny, a friend of the eleven men, referred the men to an attorney named Michael Rosenbaum who happens to be Kenny's old college buddy. When the eleven men arrive at Rosenbaum's office and enter the conference room to discuss the class action lawsuit, the men are shocked when they realize that Michael Rosenbaum is Nigerian. They all greet him with a "Hello," but their eyes reveal much more.

What is your 55% communicating through your eye expressions? Do you give people a bad look when you do not like or are uncomfortable with their diversity? Can customers tell what kind of customer service their server is about to provide as they approach their table in the restaurant? Customers most often look at the eyes and facial expressions of their servers to predict what their experience will be like in any given restaurant or hotel.

(3) Gestures

Can your arms, fingers and hand motions offend someone you are communicating and interacting with? Most definitely! Our gestures, if used inappropriately or unintentionally, can lead to major conflict and communication problems. Your gestures can communicate your attitude, emotional state and mindset. *Gestures are non-verbal motions that consist of movements of the arms, fingers and hands.*

If you are frustrated and irritated while conversing with someone, your gestures can communicate unintentional behaviors, which could lead to conflict and tension. Please analyze the following examples of how inappropriate gesturing can lead to possible misunderstandings and interpersonal conflict:

- Folding your arms in a defensive manner during a conversation.

- Fiddling with your arms, hands and fingers while someone is talking.

- Cracking your knuckles.

- Clenching your fist.

- Pointing in an aggressive, authoritative, degrading and demeaning manner.

- Using an extremely aggressive and firm handshake during a first encounter.

- Using a very weak and flimsy handshake during a first encounter.

Let Your Arms and Hands Do the Talking!

Andrea has been a bank teller at We Are the World Bank for ten years. Over the past year, Andrea has noticed that more immigrants are banking at her bank. This creates a diversity challenge for Andrea because she is experiencing communication problems and language barriers due to the thick accents and different dialects being spoken. Andrea's patience is wearing thin. Andrea becomes frustrated one day after an immigrant customer mistakenly fills out a savings deposit slip instead of a checking deposit slip. She tells the woman that she needs to fill out a checking deposit slip and the immigrant customer does not quickly grasp what Andrea is saying. Out of frustration, Andrea throws her arms and hands up in the air and points in an aggressive manner to the area of the bank where the checking deposit slips are located and says sternly, "THE CHECKING DEPOSIT SLIPS ARE RIGHT OVER THERE, MA'AM!"

During stressful times, it is very easy to allow your 55% to get the best of you. Think of a time when you used gestures inappropriately and unprofessionally. Make a list of positive gestures as well as negative gestures. The goal of this exercise is to become more aware of the gestures you use in everyday conversation. Ultimately, you want to use gestures to communicate positively to create a diversity-friendly, inclusive and welcoming environment.

(4) Posture

Posture is a non-verbal motion that explains the positioning of one's body. Consider how your posture affects your communication when interacting with diverse people. Does your posture exhibit a diversity-friendly or unfriendly demeanor? Do you find your posture more inviting and enthusiastic when communicating and interacting with certain kinds of diverse people? Whether most people admit it or not, we perk up and sit up straight when we have a high level of affinity toward the diversity we are interacting with. We can also appear slouchy, uninterested and unwilling when we interact with diversity where there is a low level of affinity.

Our affinity level does influence the way our 55% is communicated through our posture. Body orientation explains how human beings use posture to start, stop and prevent a conversation from occurring. *Body orientation is how we position our bodies during diversity encounters.* Do you face the individual you are communicating and interacting with, or do you turn away from them to stop or prevent a dialogue from occurring?

In a Stanford University study between white interviewers and black job applicants, the interviewers exhibited negative body orientation when they sat further away from the black job applicants during the actual job interview. Posturing by way of using body orientation is another example of a Microinequity and negative Micromessage. Our posture towards an individual can communicate to her or him that they are wanted or unwanted or acceptable or unacceptable. Make a list of the positive and negative kinds of posturing you could use when communicating and interacting with diverse people. The goal of this exercise is to become aware of the kinds of postures you use in everyday interactions. The ultimate goal is to use the kinds of non-verbal postures that create diversity-friendly, inclusive and welcoming environments.

Behavioral Skill #2
Be Aware of and Self-Monitor Your 38%

Please complete the following exercise to determine what tone of voice you possess.

Which Tone of Voice Do You Possess?

Please circle the answer that best represents your voice tonality that you use most often when communicating and interacting with diverse people.

Do you possess a:

(1)   **Professional** or **Unprofessional** tone of voice?

(2)   **Respectful** or **Disrespectful** tone of voice?

(3)   **Welcoming** or **Unwelcoming** tone of voice?

(4)   **Affirming** or **Disaffirming** tone of voice?

(5)   **Pleasant** or **Unpleasant** tone of voice?

(6)   **Inviting** or **Uninviting** tone of voice?

(7)   **Apathetic** or **Empathetic** tone of voice?

(8)   **Condescending** or **Uplifting** tone of voice?

(9)   **Patient** or **Impatient** tone of voice?

(10) **Sarcastic** or **Sincere** tone of voice?

(11) **Kind** or **Unkind** tone of voice?

(12) **Approving** or **Disapproving** tone of voice?

(13) **Cooperative** or **Uncooperative** tone of voice?

When my tone of voice was perceived as harsh, unkind or rude, by my mother, she would respond by saying, "J.D., don't use that tone of voice with me," or "J.D., is that tone of voice necessary to get your point across?" The tone of voice you use in everyday conversation accounts for 38% of how your message is received and understood by diverse people. Your 38% speaks volumes when you are communicating and interacting with diverse people. Successful communicators self-monitor their 38% consistently and habitually to ensure they are landing appropriate and respectful messages. Remember, communication can be intentional or unintentional. As an effective communicator, you want to avoid unintentional communication, which is a huge barrier to effective communication.

Why should you self-monitor your 38%? Self-monitoring your 38% means you are paying close attention to the emotional tone of your voice and adjusting your 38% accordingly and when necessary. For example, if a part of your career requires telephone time with employees and customers, and you know that you become easily agitated and frustrated when conversing with callers who have different accents and dialects, it is imperative that you become aware of and self-monitor your 38%. This will help to ensure that you are communicating with cooperation, empathy, kindness, warmth and respect. There are two kinds of self-monitors— high self-monitors and low self-monitors. High self-monitors are perfectly aware of their professional and unprofessional communication habits. High self-monitors ask themselves:

- What is my 38% communicating right now?

- I think my tone of voice was really rude yesterday during our team outing. How do I stop sounding so condescending when I am angry?

- Why was my 38% so cynical and sarcastic the other day?

- What can I do to ensure that I do not come off sounding rude and disrespectful?

- What can I do to ensure I use my 38% to motivate, inspire and uplift others?

Additionally, high self-monitors are aware of their Diversity BAPS, and they make sure their Diversity BAPS do not negatively affect their 38% when communicating and interacting with diverse people. It is imperative that we become familiar with our Diversity BAPS to prevent destructive communication from occurring. You will find that you will have to work just a little harder at keeping your tone of voice positive when you are experiencing diversity anxiety and discomfort. If you want to be successful with diverse people, incorporate the practical skill of becoming aware of and self-monitoring your 38% in all that you do.

Low self-monitors are the opposite of high self-monitors because they rarely, if at all, self-monitor their 38% when communicating and interacting with diverse people. You can easily identify a low self-monitor by their diversity attitude (DA) and their Diversity BAPS because of how they communicate their 38%. You will

> "It takes a disciplined person to listen to convictions
> which are different from their own."
> **Dorothy Fuldheim**

often notice that low self-monitors make more communication mistakes because they very rarely monitor their 38%. Unprofessional, disrespectful, unwelcoming, unpleasant, condescending, impatient, rude, unkind and sarcastic are just a few adjectives to describe the tone of voice low self-monitors may employ when communicating and interacting with diverse people. You may be wondering why I used such harsh adjectives to describe low self-monitors. When you do not self-monitor your 38% when communicating and interacting with diverse people, it is easy to offend them.

Research shows that high self-monitors make less communication mistakes than low self-monitors. Adler, Proctor and Towne say of low self-monitors, " …low self-monitors may blunder through life, succeeding or failing without understanding why. High self-monitors have the detachment to ask themselves the question, 'How am I doing?' Additionally, high self-monitors change their behavior if the answer is not positive." Please add the practical skill of self-monitoring your 38% to your Communication and Diversity Toolbox to ensure successful communication when interacting with diverse people.

Make Your 38% Congruent with Your Diversity Attitude (DA)

Your 38%, whether intentional or unintentional, communicates your diversity attitude and comfort level when communicating and interacting with diverse people. Remember the three kinds of diversity attitudes: apathy, sympathy and empathy. Which kind of diversity attitude do you communicate in your 38%?

When communicating and interacting with diverse people, they will try to figure out where you stand with regards to their diversity. For example, they may be thinking the following about you:

• Is she or he racist, sexist or homophobic?

• I wonder if she or he likes white people.

• I wonder if she or he is for or against interracial relationships or marriages.

- Does she or he think I received my position or promotion due to Affirmative Action?

- Will she or he really hire or promote someone who is gay and "out" regarding their sexual orientation?

Beyond their thoughts about you, the diverse person will listen and pay close attention to your 38% when you are addressing and responding to diversity-related issues and topics. They will assess the emotional tone of your 38% to get a feel for your diversity perspective and position.

Diverse people might also analyze your emotional tone. Your emotional tone is compromised of two components: (1) The volume of your voice when communicating and interacting with diverse people and (2) The number of pauses or vocal fillers you use when communicating and interacting with diverse people. Let us examine each of these components, which comprise an individual's emotional tone.

(1) Voice Volume and Pitch

All communicators possess a softness or loudness in their voice that indicates their natural communication style and expression. Your natural softness or loudness is not an issue. To communicate effectively, you need to focus on and avoid using your voice volume as a destructive tool to belittle, embarrass, demean or disrespect diverse people. Talking too softly or loudly when you dislike, resent or hate someone's unique diversity communicates your diversity attitude as well as your Diversity BAPS. Using your 38% to treat diverse people unfairly is the pathway to discrimination and poor communication.

Whether you are a teacher, doctor, lawyer, sales associate or police officer or in any other profession where you serve clients and customers, the effectiveness or ineffectiveness of how you use your voice volume and pitch will determine whether or not diverse people perceive you as diversity welcoming or diversity unwelcoming. Remember to match your 38% and voice volume and pitch with the correct diversity attitude.

Do diverse people hear excitement, energy and enthusiasm in your 38%? What words or phrases do you emphasize with your 38% while conversing with diverse people? Consider the dominant disposition you convey in your 38% every single day.

(2) Vocalized Pauses and Vocal Fillers

We communicate with more confidence and ease with individuals we know and with the diversity we feel most comfortable around. When we are in an environment where the diversity is new for us, our diversity anxiety and discomfort increases. When you are communicating and interacting with diverse people and you feel uncomfortable with their diversity, the diversity anxiety and discomfort negatively affects our 38%. When you are nervous and uncomfortable during the communication process, you tend to communicate with more apprehension, hesitation and reluctance. Diverse people can hear the second-guessing in your voice (your 38%) as you pause.

We make more speech errors when the emotions of fear, intimidation and trepidation are present. Vocalized pauses and vocal fillers occur during the communication process when we experience nervousness and high levels of anxiety. Instead of communicating intentionally the words, ideas and thoughts we desire, we unintentionally communicate with filler words and phrases such as: ah, uh, umm, hmm, err, you-know, I mean and it's like. These vocalized pauses and vocal fillers are disturbing speech errors in the communication process. Too many of these speech errors during diversity encounters and interactions will definitely send mixed messages. Do you sound like you are afraid of the diverse person you are communicating with? Vocalized pauses and vocal fillers can make you appear diversity-unfriendly and unwelcoming.

What do your speech errors (your 38%) communicate to diverse people? This is a tricky question to answer, but speech errors can be perceived in many ways. Consistent speech errors make you appear less credible and untrustworthy. In the Stanford University study referenced earlier, the white interviewers made more speech errors with the black interviewees than with the white interviewees and ended the job interview 25% sooner with the black interviewees than with the white interviewees. Does an individual's DA (diversity attitude) and Diversity BAPS affect their 38% when communicating and interacting with diverse people? Absolutely!

Behavioral Skill #3
Practice the Platinum Rule

I was seven years old and as Christmas Day approached, I was excited to see if Santa Claus had honored my Christmas wish list. I frantically opened the Christmas wrapping paper as I opened each gift. "Wow! Santa was great to me this year," I thought as I tore through one gift box in particular. It was a gift that I viewed as quite unusual since I hadn't requested it from Santa. It was a poster of a group of ethnically diverse children playing with one another on a school playground with words at the top of the poster reading, "The Golden Rule: Do Unto Others as You Would Have Others Do Unto You." I was hoping my 55% did not display signs of disapproval or disrespect as I tried my best not to reveal in my body language that I was not as excited about this gift as I were with my other gifts.

My mother had drilled the message of showing appreciation, gratitude and thankfulness inside my head ever since I could remember, so I knew I was expected to show appreciation and respect whenever I received any sort of gift from anyone (especially a gift from Santa)! I did not hate the Golden Rule poster; let's just say I did not know how to appreciate the gift at the time. At seven, the Golden Rule did not make much sense to me. However, it did not prevent my mother from reminding me of the Golden Rule before she passed away. My mother was notorious for saying, "J.D. do unto others as you would have others do you. You've got to treat people the way you want to be treated."

I thought the Golden Rule was a concept and practice that my mother had crafted and created, but with age, time and experience, I realized the Golden Rule was deeply ingrained in the American culture. The Golden Rule philosophy is taught and endorsed by many walks of faith. This familiar phrase instructs us to treat other people the way we would want to be treated. This rule does not take into account the different and unique needs of each individual person we communicate and interact with. The Golden Rule essentially implies that other people in the world would like to be treated in the exact fashion as we would like to be treated. In a world with over six billion human beings, it is unfair to assume that other people are just like *you*, want to be like *you* or should be like *you*. Treating a person, as you would like to be treated denies people of their individuality, personal expectations and unique diversity.

In regards to the Golden Rule, editor of the book, *Basic Concepts of Intercultural Communication,* Dr. Milton Bennett writes:

> *"The Golden Rule is typically used as a kind of template for behavior. If I am unsure of how to treat you, I simply imagine how I myself would like to be treated, and then act in accordance. The positive value of this form of the Rule is virtually axiomatic in U.S. American culture, and so its underlying assumption frequently goes unstated: other people want to be treated as I do. And under this assumption lies another, more pernicious belief: all people are basically the same, and thus they really should want the same treatment (whether they admit it or not) as I would.*
>
> *Simply stated, the Golden Rule in this form does not work because people are actually different from one another. Not only are they individually different, but also they are systematically different in terms of national culture, ethnic group, socioeconomic status, age, gender, sexual orientation, political allegiance, educational background, and profession, to name but a few possibilities. Associated with these differences in people are differences in values—values which cannot easily be generalized to all people from those of any given group."*

I am a definite proponent of the Golden Rule when applied appropriately. I advocate using the Golden Rule *only* in the spirit of consideration, as it is a remarkable principle with regard to showing appreciation, concern, common cordiality, gratitude, respect and thankfulness to one another. If the Golden Rule is applied verbatim, it can create communication barriers during diversity encounters and cross-cultural interactions.

Diversity conflict and tension occurs because the Golden Rule makes the assumption that everyone desires the same sort of treatment. For example, to adhere to the practical application of the Golden Rule means I would treat every single person I encounter as though they were exactly like me, Jermaine M. Davis. Of course, this would be a colossal assumption to make because there are billions of people who would not like to be treated like Jermaine M. Davis. Therefore, I am much more diversity competent and effective as a communicator if I treat individuals the way *they* would like to be treated. The philosophy and practice of diversity competence teaches: discover how individuals would prefer to be treated and treat them according to their desires. This rule of engagement will increase your ability to get along with diverse people.

When we treat others the way *we* want to be treated according to our personal preferences, we communicate a lack of consideration for others in three important areas. First, there is a *disregard of people's unique differences as well as their cultural beliefs, cultural influences and cultural practices.* People may not want to be treated the way *you* want to treat them. To treat a Muslim as a Christian or a Christian as an Atheist would definitely lead to communication conflict and diversity tension.

Secondly, the use of *your* personal preference as a measurement of how to appropriately treat people does not take into account the *personal preferences of other people.* People have their own personal preferences as to how they like to be treated as individuals. I often tell my communication students that they will be effective communicators if they discover what people prefer and adjust their communication approach and style accordingly. For example, to force someone to shake your hand that prefers to bow during a greeting will ensure some sort of diversity conflict and tension.

Third, when we treat others the way we want to be treated, there is *disregard of the fact that people as human beings are different, which is the basis and foundation of diversity.* Should women treat men as women and men treat women as men? I think not. Men are men and women are women. Sometimes in male-dominated organizations and industries, diversity incompetent men will try to include the new female colleague by trying to treat her as one of the guys. The philosophy and practice of diversity

> "Treat people
> the way they would
> like or prefer
> to be treated."
> **The Platinum Rule**

competence does not support this well-intentioned practice.

I recommend that individuals live by and practice the Platinum Rule in every personal, professional and private relationship. This diversity competent skill encourages that individuals do their diversity and intercultural homework when communicating and interacting with diverse people. This means finding out how the diverse people you are communicating and interacting with prefer to be treated and vice versa. When you discover their preferred style of engagement, you increase your probability of connecting with them personally and professionally.

Dr. Tony Alessandra and Dr. Michael O'Connor define The Platinum Rule as, "Do unto others as *they'd* like done unto them." They write in their book *The Platinum Rule*, "That means in short, learning to really understand other people—and then handling them in a way that's best for *them*, not just for us. It means taking the time to figure out the people around us, and then adjusting our behavior to make them more comfortable. It means using our knowledge and our tact to try to put others at ease. That we suggest, is the true spirit of The Golden Rule. So **The Platinum Rule** is not at odds with The Golden Rule. Instead, you might say it's a newer, more sensitive version."

The Platinum Rule communicates that you accept the fact that people are different from you. It implies that you respect other people's differences enough to treat them how they prefer to be treated.

Behavioral Skill #4
STOP Offensive Comments and Inappropriate Behaviors

Have you ever been at a loss for words when you needed a few words to bring justice to an offensive conversation? Have you ever needed words to rectify an uncomfortable atmosphere created by inappropriate language and unprofessional behaviors? Have you ever wanted to stop classmates in school or colleagues in the workplace who make offensive comments?

Some examples of offensive comments include:

- "So you like dating those kinds of people."

- "You don't sound black to me."

- "You know all men are sexist pigs."

- "Oh, there goes the neighborhood now."

- "Gays and lesbians are promiscuous."

- "Religious people are so conservative and close-minded."

- "Come on, you know how blondes are."

- "I guess I'll have to learn a new language if they keep hiring those kind of people."

- "Women are overly emotional, hysterical and loose cannons."

- "They look like 'fags,' 'faggots,' 'sissies' and 'lesbos.'"

Responding to these kinds of statements can be both awkward and exhausting. Most often people tell me that they do not say anything to address statements like these in the workplace or school environments. Those who do respond do so in an inappropriate manner, using aggressive communication while simultaneously acting out of control in an emotional manner. Typically, this communication approach does not stop or minimize the offensive comments; it worsens it, leading to more diversity conflict and tension.

Why are some people members of the silent majority club while others are members of the outspoken minority club? Diversity fear, diversity discomfort and lack of conflict management skills are the three barriers that separate those who represent the silent majority and the outspoken minority.

Some individuals who are not aware of the power of communication believe silence has no communicative value. This is a HUGE myth and fallacy. Silence *is* a great communicator. Silence speaks volumes and communicates approval or disapproval, whether you are for or against a decision, acceptance or non-acceptance. Some individuals believe that it is easier to just sit still and be quiet. They may be correct if they possess a DA (diversity attitude) of sympathy or apathy and they represent the part of the organization I referred to earlier as **The Middle 80%**—The Diversity NIMBYs (Not In My Back Yard). When an individual sits still and silent in the midst of offensive comments and inappropriate behaviors, she or he communicates to diverse people that they agree with the offender's offensive comments and inappropriate behaviors.

A very effective communication tool in the field of diversity is the **STOP Model** (defined below). The following scenarios are examples that illustrate how to best use the **STOP Model** in life, school and work. Please commit to practicing and memorizing this step-by-step process to increase your diversity competence.

State: *State* What You *Heard* or *Observed* in an Objective Manner.

The first thing to do is to make sure you are mentally and emotionally ready to respond to offensive comments and inappropriate behaviors. Sometimes it is not wise to address difficult issues if you feel emotionally unable to (i.e., you are extremely angry, frustrated or irritated). Going forward with this will only lead to uncontrollable explosions and outbursts, which you will regret later. Proceed with difficult dialogue when you feel emotionally ready (i.e., you are calm, have cooled down and have collected your thoughts rationally). Once you are ready, you can address the offender regarding her or his offensive comments and inappropriate behaviors in an objective, respectful, non-threatening and non-defensive manner.

Remember, maintaining objectivity is the key to preventing defensive behaviors and responses in others. The best approach to maintaining objectivity is to use "I" language or statements when addressing sensitive diversity issues. When a communicator uses "I" language or statements, it communicates to the individual that you are taking responsibility for the message that you are sending. An example of an "I" statement is: "I felt offended when you made that comment about Judaism because I am Jewish." The opposite is "You" messages and statements, where the communicator expresses judgment about the offender's comments and behaviors. An example of a "You" statement is: "You must be some type of Nazi because you always say negative things about Jewish people."

I understand that you will experience frustration, hurt and anger. I would like you to remember that there is one important principle to always keep in mind when communicating and interacting with diverse people: communication can be *intentional* or *unintentional*. Sometimes we offend one another in the communication process and it is truly unintentional, which means that the comments and behaviors were not premeditated with the intention to cause harm, destruction and defeat. Yes, offensive comments need to be altered and inappropriate behaviors need to change, but I suggest you assume others have good intentions until proven guilty or experienced otherwise.

*T*ell: *Tell* the Offender How You *Feel* as a Result of What She or He *Said* or *Did*.

As communicators, we have what I refer to as communication blind spots. *Communication blind spots are verbal and non-verbal communication habits, which other people can see, but are unknown and invisible to you while communicating and interacting with diverse people.* We learn of our communication blind spots when diverse people make them known to us. As communicators, we have both positive and negative communication blind spots that we are totally unaware of as individuals. If diverse people are concerned and caring colleagues, customers, friends and family members, they pay us a great service when they make our communication blind spots known to us. If they choose not to share our communication blind spots with us, we go through life, school and work offending diverse people and destroying personal, professional and private relationships without knowing the real reasons. How unfortunate!

Why should you tell the offender how you feel regarding their offensive comments and inappropriate behaviors? There are three reasons why you should do so.

Reason #1: To make them aware of their comments and behaviors because they may not be aware of their offensive comments and inappropriate behaviors due to their communication blind spots.

Reason #2: To provide them with a chance and opportunity to change or stop their offensive comments and inappropriate behaviors.

Reason #3: (the core of step number two in the **STOP Model**): The offender needs to know how her or his comments and behaviors have impacted your *feelings*.

Why does the offender need to be made aware of your feelings and your emotional state as a result of their offensive comments and inappropriate behaviors? Put simply, offenders need to know the magnitude of their comments and behaviors. Communicating and revealing your emotional status to the offender lets them know how deeply you were wounded. You want them to know how their comments and behaviors registered on your emotional Richter scale. Did their comments and behaviors register as high, medium or low? If the offender does not know the severity of your emotional pain and mental anguish, she or he will not be motivated to stop offending you with offensive comments and inappropriate behaviors in the future.

*O*ptions: Provide the Offender with *Optional* Ways of Communicating and Behaving.

It may not be enough to tell someone who has offended you with words and actions to stop if you want her or him to permanently stop offending you and others. People need optional and alternative ways of communicating and behaving when they have been told their current communication and behavioral styles are offensive and inappropriate. They need time to replace old behaviors with new behaviors. This is where the offended person and the offender can work on effective ways of communicating and appropriate ways of behaving together. This is the ultimate win-win situation.

For example, I describe a woman that I work with as "Native," and she overhears my description of her and is appalled and offended because she deems my adjective to be inappropriate. She proceeds by telling my manager that I need diversity training because I referred to her as "Native," and she says she is not Native. She tells my manager, "I want him to stop offending me and my people with derogatory names and adjectives." Now, I feel bad that I have unintentionally offended her, and I dislike that my manager is involved. However, her disappointment with me and my manager's awareness of the situation does not provide me with the appropriate communication skills to correct the present situation, which leaves me at risk to offend someone again. My colleague needs to provide me with alternative descriptors, such as "Native American," "American Indian," "Indigenous People" or other adjectives that she finds appropriate. We can only fix a broken situation when we have the correct and proper tools. Provide people with options to ensure they know how to correct their offensive comments and inappropriate behaviors.

*P*rovide *P*ersonal and *P*rofessional Benefits: The Bottom Line is that People want to Know W.I.I.F.M. *(What's In It For Me)*.

It is easier for individuals to change when they can see how the change will personally and professionally benefit them. Show them how stopping their offensive comments and inappropriate behaviors will benefit them both personally and professionally. Sometimes individuals will only stop communicating and behaving offensively and inappropriately in their professional lives because they can see how their comments and behaviors can interfere with their career, reputation (workplace) and upward mobility. However, they may decide to *not* make any changes in their personal life. The goal is to communicate to the offenders how they can benefit from replacing their offensive comments and inappropriate behaviors with more appropriate comments and behaviors, so that they make it a life practice as well as a workplace practice.

Here are a few examples to outline how to best use the **STOP Model**:

Scenario	Ricky calls Ronny "gay" after Ronny hugged another man named Ryan.	I was riding in the back seat of a car when my friends and I passed a group of Asian Americans in another vehicle. The driver remarked, "Look at all those Chinks."
State	"Ricky, I believe I overheard you call Ronny 'gay' after he gave Ryan a hug. Did I hear you correctly?"	"I am surprised by your comment when I heard you refer to the Asian Americans as, 'Chinks.' Did I hear you correctly?"

Tell	"I was offended when I heard you refer to Ronny as 'gay' after he gave Ryan a hug. I don't believe a man is gay because he hugs another man or shows his affections towards a male friend. I think your comment was offensive and inappropriate."	"I don't know what you meant by that, but I found it offensive that you referred to the Asian Americans as 'Chinks.'" "The word 'Chink' is a very degrading, derogatory and disrespectful word. I'm extremely hurt because that communicated disdain towards an entire group of people. I am equally offended because my best friend is Asian American."
Options	"What did you mean when you said that Ronny was 'gay?' Were you just joking around? Do you know what his sexual orientation actually is? Were you saying that as an insult? Can you explain to me how you determine a man's sexual orientation by whether or not he touches members of the same gender? Please explain why you said that, and what you really meant." "Ricky, I think a more appropriate description of Ronny's behavior is, 'Ronny is very affectionate towards his male friends as well as his female friends.'" "Wow, I didn't know that Ronny was as affectionate as he is."	"I realize that you may have simply meant that they appear to be Chinese, which is perfectly okay, but the word you used and the way it was used made me feel uncomfortable as if you didn't like Asian Americans. It seemed to me that you were insulting Asian Americans for no reason, and that you were suggesting that there is something wrong with being Chinese or Asian. What did you mean by that?" "If you are not sure of an Asian American's specific ethnic origin, it is both respectful and safer to say 'Asian American' or ask the members of your group what they perceive as the ethnic origin of the group you are attempting to describe or identify."

Personal and Professional Benefits	"It's really important that we create a diversity-friendly, inclusive and welcoming environment for all employees. I would prefer that you not use sexual orientation as an insult. I don't think it's fair to people, whatever their sexual orientation is." "Offensive comments in the workplace can lead to diversity conflict and tension, which can lead to the organization losing talented and valuable employees to competition." "I found it inappropriate that you seemed to jump to a conclusion about a man's sexual orientation based upon innocent nonsexual physical contact. This can be perceived as discrimination, which could cost the organization millions of dollars and cost you your career. I would appreciate it if in the future you do not do that. I want all employees to feel safe around here. Thanks!"	"Perhaps you are used to describing Chinese or Asian Americans as 'Chinks'. I suggest that you show respect and regard toward all humanity by using appropriate language." "You never know who you are around, what their values are or what their family and friend's backgrounds are, so avoid making assumptions that all people share your perspective on diversity and diversity-related issues."

Using the **STOP Model** and addressing offensive comments and inappropriate behaviors takes "diversity courage." What is diversity courage? ***Diversity courage is the mental, emotional and physical strength to face your diversity fears*** *and challenges head-on.* There will be times when you will have to pick and choose your diversity battles. Do you fight every single offensive comment and inappropriate behavior in life, school and work? Here is an even more challenging question—do you have the time, energy and resources to fight every offensive comment and inappropriate behavior? There will be times when you must address diversity issues immediately, and there will be times when you will have to pull the person aside and practice the **STOP Model** in a quiet area in the office with that one person. Communication and conflict research does advocate taking the person aside and discussing the issue in private. When individuals are confronted in front of other people, it increases the chances of a defensive response or behavior. When human beings feel threatened, even if what you are communicating to her or him is correct, they will attempt to preserve their pride and dignity in the midst of other people. In my book *Leading with Greatness*, I wrote that when providing feedback to others remember to criticize in *private* and praise in *public*.

Diversity Courage: The Branch Rickey Sr. Story

Mr. Branch Rickey was a Major League Baseball executive who, despite common convention, chose to think outside of the box. The era in which he was an executive – the mid 1940s – no man of color had played major league baseball since 1887 (This was a fact even though there were no legal sanctions against it; it just was not done due to the institution of racism). Branch Rickey saw baseball as a sport that was quickly becoming a major national pastime and people from all backgrounds and races were becoming interested in the sport of baseball.

Mr. Rickey had never met anyone in the major league who was not white, but he knew plenty of African-Americans and Latinos who played, and knew how to play the game. He decided it was time that the major league was integrated for all to play and enjoy. On April 16, 1945, Boston City Councilman Isadore Muchnick auditioned the first three African-American ball players—Marvin Williams, Sam Jethroe and the now famous Jackie Robinson. While the Red Sox did not pick anyone up, Jackie Robinson was such a good player that he demanded the attention of Branch Rickey, who eventually signed Jackie Robinson to the Brooklyn Dodgers. This decision was not without diversity conflict and tension.

The integration of people of color into the game of baseball was not easy, and it took two years before Jackie Robinson actually played for the Dodgers. Nevertheless, the color barrier was finally broken in the sport of baseball. Branch later signed a Latino player, Roberto Clemente. None of this was done without controversy, but Rickey was motivated by idealism and equality and felt there should be no reason to separate the blacks and whites in baseball. Jackie Robinson went on to become Rookie of the Year and paved the way for other people of color to join him in the playing of major league sports of all types.

Branch Rickey showed a great deal of "diversity courage." He saw an opportunity that depended on breaking generally accepted ways of doing things and took a stand on something he believed in. Even today, there are opportunities and places for diversity courage. America has not yet fixed all the problems regarding diversity issues, including racism, sexism and homophobia. Sometimes it just takes one or two individuals to break through a barrier for others to follow their lead. Where, in your life, do you see "diversity courage" just waiting to happen? If you see it, that is a wonderful thing. If you choose to do something about it, that is a courageous thing.

Behavioral Skill #5
Check Your Diversity Perceptions

Checking your diversity perceptions is a communication and diversity tool to help individuals understand diverse people and situations more accurately. It also helps individuals to avoid making assumptions of diverse people and cultures. People tend to believe that their first interpretation is 100% accurate. However, this is not the case all the time, which can lead to communication breakdowns and misunderstandings. Checking your diversity perceptions when you are unsure of how to read and interpret a diversity encounter or interaction can significantly reduce if not eliminate diversity conflict and tension. This wonderful tool prevents you from making assumptions, over-reacting and jumping to conclusions.

There are three components to Checking Your Diversity Perceptions, based on Adler, Proctor and Towne's book, *Looking Out Looking In*:

(1) Provide a description of the behavior you observed.

(2) Provide two interpretations of the person's behavior.

(3) Request a clarification on how to interpret the person's behavior.

Here is an example of how you can check your diversity perceptions.

Is He Islamophobic or Just Rude?

Scenario:

Gina, a manager within her organization, is describing a new employee she hired to several of her colleagues who are also managers. Her colleague, Brad, wants to know if Gina's new employee is Muslim. Gina responds, "Yes, his religion is Islam." Brad replies, "So I see you feel comfortable hiring Muslims, huh?" as he gets up from his chair during the middle of the conversation and walks out of the employee break room. Gina and the two remaining colleagues are trying to figure out Brad's erratic behavior.

Gina and her two colleagues may accurately or inaccurately interpret Brad's comment and behavior. They can assume they understand Brad, but are they 100% sure what Brad meant by his statement and his actions? The most effective way to make sense of Brad's comment and behavior is for Gina and her colleagues to practice the communication and diversity skill of checking their diversity perceptions for accuracy.

Solution:

(1) Gina can provide a description of the behavior she noticed to Brad:

"Brad, help me understand the situation that took place during lunch in the break room. I was describing my new employee, and after I confirmed your question as to whether or not he was Muslin, you got up from your chair and walked out of the employee break room while the conversation was still going on."

(2) Gina can provide two interpretations of Brad's comment and behavior:

"I wasn't sure if you had to run to a meeting or use the restroom and that was the reason you left so abruptly."

"I began to wonder if you have issues with Islam, and with the fact that our organization hires Muslims."

(3) Gina could request a clarification from Brad of how to interpret and make sense out of his comment and behavior:

"Can you explain to me why you left so abruptly, so I won't interpret your behaviors inaccurately?"

When individuals do not use or do not know how to check their diversity perceptions, many diversity-related issues get misinterpreted and described as racist, sexist, homophobic and discriminatory. It is possible that individuals can perceive unfair situations as acts of discrimination when in fact these acts are simply a benign misunderstanding. Practicing this diversity skill and incorporating it into your daily communication and interaction style can reduce diversity conflict and tension in life, school and work.

Behavioral Skill #6
Practice Diversity Forgiveness

The Day I Got Beat Up

It was October, 16, 1995, and one of my best friends, Tumchee Howard, was visiting from Chicago. It was a special day for African-Americans and their allies throughout the United States. It was the Day of Atonement, the Day of the Million Man March. I had taken the day off from teaching as a fifth and sixth grade teacher to honor the events of the day. Throughout the day, Tumchee and I watched the Million Man March on television while engaging in deep, philosophical discussions about the state of the black community and black men and brainstorming ideas for strategies to uplift communities of color.

Later that evening, I decided to take Tumchee, who enjoys a beer every now and then, out for a celebratory cocktail. While I do not drink beer, this was the last night of Tumchee's visit, and I had heard from a teaching colleague about a specialty bar and grill with a great selection of imported beer. In fact, the offerings there were so extensive the bartenders would even educate patrons on the different types of beers and their histories. Once at the bar, we stood in line conversing while waiting to get inside.

Finally, at the front of the line, the bouncer handed back my ID he'd just checked and stated, "I can't let you into the establishment. Your pants are too saggy."

I couldn't believe it. I glanced down at my medium blue Khakis. While not tight-fitting, they were nowhere near sagging as he'd suggested. "Please, look at my pants, sir," I asked. I was sure he'd made a visual mistake. "They're not saggy, sir," I assured him.

The door-bouncer paid no attention to my request and he repeated, "Get out of line, sir; I cannot allow you into the establishment."

I moved aside, not believing what was happening. My embarrassment was quite evident to anyone looking my way because I was having difficulty keeping my true feelings inside. Determined to show my best friend a good time during his last night in town, I replied, "I would like to speak to a manager."

Without looking at me he said, "There's no manager on duty, sir."

Managing to suppress my own rising anger, I insisted, "C'mon, man, I know there's a manager on duty."

The door-bouncer exchanged words with another bouncer who went inside the bar and returned with a man who said he was the manager of the bar.

I was certain this gentleman would resolve the situation and restore justice promptly. I explained, "I'm a grade school teacher, and I'm not here to cause any problems. I just want to show my best friend a great time on his last night in town. I'm having problems being admitted into your establishment because one of your bouncers said my pants are too saggy. Yet, while standing here, I've observed six white men wearing pants that were saggier than my pants and they were admitted into your establishment."

Escalating Emotions

Without warning, the manager's facial expression hardened and he blurted, "Oh, f*** you! Are you turning this into a racial situation? Are you playing the f***ing race card? Don't pull this bullshit with me!"

My own anger raging now, I replied mindlessly, "No, f*** you, and I'm not playing the race card, sir. I'm only sharing my observations!"

I turned away from the manager, knowing after the heated verbal exchange, that my admittance into the bar was not going to happen. Tumchee and I began walking to my car. I didn't get very far before I was grabbed and tackled from behind. Within moments, four bouncers were pressing me down to the ground and scraping my face against the asphalt in the process. There was no use turning to my friend for help because two other bouncers had him pinned and locked up too. When they lifted me from the ground, I was dripping blood from open wounds on my face, shoulder and left elbow.

The police were called and when they arrived, we were placed in a squad car, but not handcuffed. Driving from the scene the policeman asked what happened. When I finished detailing the entire evening, the officer turned and said, "Mr. Davis, you sound like an intelligent guy."

Without hesitation, I stated, "I am. I'm an educated young man, officer!"

The officer said, "You know what? I believe every word of your story, and I'm going to let you go." And he did. He let me out of his patrol car, right in the heart of downtown Minneapolis, one block away from the police station.

As my Uncle Ricky did, I could have allowed that moment to color and shape my perceptions of white people, but I deliberately and intentionally did not. I chose to deal with my anger and the incident constructively and in a healthy manner. Though I reflected on the infamous words of my Uncle Ricky, I immediately refuted those irrational thoughts and debilitative emotions.

Can you forgive someone when you hear a colleague, classmate or neighbor refer to your diversity with labels such as: "redneck honkies," "niggers," "chinks," "wetbacks," "gooks," "faggots," "bitches," "crackers" and so on? Are these derogatory terms the ultimate deal breakers for you or can you forgive the person and move on without holding a grudge?

Can the black woman who was consistently passed over for career promotions in a predominantly white organization forgive? When she becomes quiet, reserved and guarded in the workplace, she's now labeled and described as an angry black woman with a negative attitude. Can she forgive and move forward?

Can the white male forgive? The one who has had his dream position postponed far too many times because the organization he works for has a diversity initiative in place to hire and retain more women and people of color. Can he forgive and embrace his colleagues who are female and people of color? Will he view them as possible career threats, leading him to only hang out with and embrace his white male colleagues?

Can the Latino man who was falsely accused of rape by the white woman forgive? She reported a man of color to the authorities because she believed her story would be far more credible and believable if she selected someone from a minority group. Later, the authorities and the Latino man discover the woman was having an affair, became pregnant and needed an alibi to justify her need for an abortion.

The Latino man of course was her scapegoat. Can the Latino man forgive her? Is it really possible?

These examples and stories are based on real life events. Is it possible for the victims in these stories to forgive those who have offended them? I often find that when I go to schools and organizations to conduct *Be Diversity Competent* workshops, hundreds and thousands of individuals are holding diversity grudges and harboring diversity resentment against one another. In my personal and professional experience, I have found that harboring diversity resentment is one of the greatest barriers to diversity competence, which prevents diverse people from communicating and interacting effectively with one another.

My personal and professional suggestion is that individuals practice diversity forgiveness. *Diversity forgiveness occurs when individuals deliberately decide to forgive those who have offended them and not to harbor diversity resentment as a result of diversity-related conflict and tension.* Harboring diversity grudges and resentment is like a deadly disease or poison that kills you from the inside out. Often when individuals hold grudges against another person, they tend to believe that they are harming the other person and paying them back. The reality, however, is that the person who is holding the grudge is doing more damage and harm to themselves because of the huge amount of mental, emotional and physical energy they are using to maintain those debilitative emotions. The poisonous grudge will mentally, emotionally and physically kill them until they release the poison from their being. The key to releasing the poisonous grudge is to practice the behavioral skill of diversity forgiveness.

Why practice diversity forgiveness? Diversity forgiveness allows you to move forward in life, school and work after a diversity-related conflict has occurred. There are two kinds of emotions that determine the success or failure rate of an individual after a diversity-related conflict has taken place. The two emotions are *facilitative* emotions and *debilitative* emotions. According to Adler, Proctor and Towne, authors of *Looking Out Looking In*, "Facilitative emotions contribute to effective functioning and debilitative emotions detract from effective functioning." One emotion helps you to move forward after a diversity-related conflict, and the other emotion prevents you from moving forward.

I have outlined the advantages and disadvantages of facilitative and debilitative emotions below.

What are the Advantages of Facilitative Emotions?

Facilitative emotions allow you to experience the full range of human emotions after you have been wronged or disrespected by someone. Allowing oneself to emote appropriately is a critical step in the healing process after an emotional injury. I always tell workshop participants that it is okay to grieve and feel anger after they have been hurt, let down or betrayed from an offensive comment or inappropriate behavior. After a diversity-related conflict has caused pain and injury, it is quite normal to feel emotional stress and mental anguish. Going somewhere quiet to yell, scream and cry is an awesome way to release tension. It is imperative that you allow your emotions to express themselves in a healthy manner. Facilitative emotions move you toward a healthy and positive state after a diversity injury has occurred. Facilitative emotions permit you to grieve, but the ultimate goal is to prevent diversity grudges and resentment from interfering with your personal and professional growth.

What are the Disadvantages of Debilitative Emotions?

Debilitative emotions stifle and interfere with your ability to move on in life, school or work after a diversity-related conflict has occurred. Diversity grudges and harboring diversity resentment are the kinds of debilitative emotions, which prevent diverse people from communicating and interacting effectively with one another. One factor that distinguishes debilitative emotions from facilitative emotions is that debilitative emotions have a longer duration. This means debilitative emotions have a tendency to wear out their welcome because they stay longer than they need to. Remember, with facilitative emotions you mourn and experience anger after a diversity conflict, but you eventually move on. People with debilitative emotions cannot move on or will not move on because they *choose* not to move on. Moving on does not imply you forget what happened to you. Moving on implies that you get on with your life and profession so you can continue to be an effective and productive person. Debilitative emotions keeps the poison inside of you, eventually killing future relationships and growth opportunities in life, school and work.

Diversity forgiveness also includes offenders forgiving themselves after they have acknowledged, admitted to and asked for forgiveness as a result of their offensive comments and inappropriate behaviors. There are cases when the offended person has forgiven the offender and moved on, but *the offender* has not forgiven herself or himself of their offensive words or inappropriate actions. This prevents them from developing a healthy diversity relationship with the diverse person they have offended because they are anchored in self-pity, embarrassment and personal and professional disappointment. When the offender is overcome with these kinds of thoughts and feelings, she or he will avoid the person they have offended and possibly group members of the diverse person's group.

Help! I've Offended Someone and I Can't Move On

For example, I make an offensive statement regarding our Vietnamese employees during a team meeting, and I unintentionally offend five of my Vietnamese colleagues. My Vietnamese colleagues professionally challenge my thoughts and ideas and they forgive me and move forward. However, I cannot move on from the diversity-related incident because I am too embarrassed and cannot believe what came out of my mouth during our team meeting. Due to my inability to accept what has happened and move on, I either limit my communication and interaction with my Vietnamese colleagues, or I simply avoid them altogether. When situations like this occur in the workplace, they destroy organizational and diversity synergy, which leads to poor productivity, stifled creativity and increased workplace conflict and tension.

You may be thinking that you cannot believe the author of this book is asking you to forgive someone who wounded you personally and professionally. You may be thinking to yourself that the person who offended you is actually racist, sexist, homophobic and an ethnocentric individual. This may be true of the person who offended you. However, holding onto diversity grudges and resentment will never allow you to build and seek diverse relationships. I have seen careers destroyed because individuals could not move forward after a diversity-related conflict occurred.

Maintaining diversity grudges and resentment is physically unhealthy for the grudge holder. Let me further explain what forgiveness is and what forgiveness is not using the professional help of Dr. Fred Luskin, Director and Cofounder of the Stanford University Forgiveness Project and author of the book, *Forgive for Good*. Dr. Luskin writes.

Forgiveness is...

• Forgiveness is for you and not the offender.

• Forgiveness is taking back your power.

• Forgiveness is taking responsibility for how you feel.

• Forgiveness is about your healing and not about the people who hurt you.

• Forgiveness is a trainable skill just like learning to throw a baseball.

• Forgiveness helps you get control over your feelings.

• Forgiveness can improve your mental and physical health.

• Forgiveness is becoming a hero instead of a victim.

• Forgiveness is a choice.

• Everyone can learn to forgive.

Forgiveness is not...

• Forgiveness is not condoning unkindness.

• Forgiveness is not forgetting that something painful happened.

• Forgiveness is not excusing poor behavior.

• Forgiveness does not have to be an otherworldly or religious experience.

• Forgiveness is not denying or minimizing your hurt.

• Forgiveness does not mean you give up having feelings.

The practice of diversity forgiveness encourages you to move from diversity chaos and conflict to diversity communication and cooperation. One of the goals of diversity forgiveness is to prevent diversity-related anger and resentment from escalating into diversity hatred. Part three of the book reminds us of how unchecked and unmonitored diversity grudges can easily turn into diversity hatred when we remember the unfortunate and gruesome deaths of James Byrd Jr. (the black man dragged to death in Jasper, Texas) and Matthew Shepard (the gay college student who was beaten to death in Laramie, Wyoming). These hate crimes first began as diversity grudges and escalated into heinous crimes.

The Health Benefits of Practicing Diversity Forgiveness

The opening story of *Be Diversity Competent* is entitled "Uncle Ricky & Me: A Missed Opportunity." This story discusses how one of my favorite uncles died diversity incompetent and a prisoner of his own Diversity BAPS (Biases, Assumptions, Prejudices and Stereotypes) because he never practiced diversity forgiveness. Uncle Ricky never overcame and forgave the group of white college men who yelled and screamed racial epithets as they jumped, kicked and punched him as he walked to his campus apartment after a night class one evening.

Uncle Ricky died with diversity anger, disgust and resentment lingering inside his mind, body and soul. When I spent time with Uncle Ricky on the weekends, I could see how this negative diversity experience had impacted him because he was never his normal self in the midst of white people. At times, Uncle Ricky was very sarcastic, cynical and abrasive as he communicated and interacted with white people.

How did holding his diversity grudge affect him? Scientific research shows that holding grudges are detrimental and hazardous to an individual's mental, emotional and physical health and well-being. Director and Cofounder of the Stanford University Forgiveness Project, Dr. Fred Luskin, reinforces the dangers of holding grudges and the negative effects of holding anger when he writes:

> *"Other studies show that people who evidence higher degrees of blame suffer more from a variety of illnesses. You will remember that blame is at the core of holding a grudge. Blaming others emerges as the result of an inability to manage anger and hurt. Medical and psychological studies have shown for years that anger and hostility are harmful to cardiovascular health. These studies show that people who have difficulty managing anger*

have higher rates of heart disease and suffer more heart attacks.

I was concerned with anger because of the research that shows anger to be a significant risk factor for heart disease. Heart disease is the leading cause of death for both men and women. A recent study looked at adults who had normal blood pressure. The subjects were given a psychological test to measure their levels of anger. Those with high levels of anger were found to be three times more likely to develop heart disease than those with low levels of anger. This is because anger causes the release of stress chemicals, which alter the functioning of your heart and cause the narrowing of your coronary and peripheral arteries."

If I could visit with Uncle Ricky one more time, I would tell him about the benefits of diversity forgiveness. I would tell Uncle Ricky that studies have found those who forgave and practiced diversity forgiveness had a decrease in blood pressure, muscle tension, physical illnesses, overall stress and heart rates when compared to those who did not practice diversity forgiveness. I would tell Uncle Ricky that the University of Wisconsin-Madison and the University of Tennessee both explored the relationship between forgiveness and its effects on the human body. Both universities found that it is in the best interest of human beings to practice diversity forgiveness to prevent diversity grudges from destroying their healthy mental, emotional and physical well-being.

As you can see, biologically and scientifically holding diversity grudges and allowing the emotion of anger to be present in one's life can be hugely destructive. Holding diversity grudges increases an individual's stress level. We experience stress as human beings when we allow certain events and issues to disturb our healthy mental, emotional and physical well-being. Are you willing to allow a negative diversity encounter and experience to anchor you in resentment or hate for the rest of your life? Are you willing to sacrifice living a healthy life as a result of holding onto a diversity grudge? Chronic, ongoing and untreated diversity stress can negatively affect your central nervous system, increase your blood pressure and leave you living a life on-edge due to constant agitation, irritation and frustration. Which will prevail in your life: diversity grudges or diversity forgiveness?

What to Do When You Have Offended Someone

In my book *Leading with Greatness*, I address the issue of reconciliation and the five steps to take when a leader desires to regain trust after she or he has betrayed colleagues and employees' trust. These five steps are applicable to resolving diversity conflict and tension if individuals are willing to practice diversity forgiveness. Please consider the five steps to rebuilding diversity trust after offensive comments or inappropriate behaviors have led to diversity conflict and tension.

The 5 Steps to Rebuilding Diversity Trust

(1) Acknowledge and admit to your offensive comment and inappropriate behavior.

To rebuild diversity trust, it is imperative that you *quickly* acknowledge and admit to your offensive comments or inappropriate behaviors. This is a clear sign of maturity and regard for the person you have offended. So what's the difference between acknowledging and admitting? ***Acknowledgement implies that you recognize how your comments or behaviors have wounded the offended person and destroyed diversity trust.*** For some individuals, this process may require reflecting on the specific incident that led to the diversity conflict and tension. The purpose of self-reflection is to recall what really took place with the goal of discovering the actual point of conflict to effectively resolve the matter. If self-reflecting does not bring you any closer to seeing how you have offended someone with your words or actions, you will need to get the offended person's perspective to help you see the impact of your words or actions.

Admitting is taking personal accountability and ownership for your offenses by verbally confessing to your unacceptable words and actions to the person you have offended. When you verbally admit to your offensive words and actions and apologize sincerely, you are perceived as authentic and humble. However, if you postpone and avoid admitting to your offenses, you will be perceived as apathetic, arrogant, self-righteous, stubborn and a few other adjectives that are not appropriate to mention in this book.

Is He Homophobic or Just Rude?

A gay couple walks into a restaurant holding hands and Jerry, the host, whispers to Glen, a server, "I can't stand freakin' faggots." Jerry does not know that Glen is actually gay and offended by his homophobic and derogatory comment. Glen is too angry to address the issue because he knows that he will explode emotionally, leading to unprofessional behavior in front of customers. He decides to share the diversity-related conflict with the manager on duty. When the manager addresses the issue with Jerry, he does not know what to say or do, so Jerry decides to avoid interacting with Glen when they work on the same shift. Both Glen and Jerry find it difficult and uncomfortable to work with one another after diversity conflict and tension has stifled their communication and interaction with one another.

What Should Jerry do to Begin the Process of Rebuilding Diversity Trust?

Jerry could acknowledge his offensive comment and say, "Glen, the comment I made the other day when the gay couple came into the restaurant was offensive and unnecessary. The manager on duty shared with me how offended you were, and I should not have made that statement."

Jerry could also admit to his offensive comment, "Glen, when I whispered in your ear, 'I can't stand freakin' faggots,' I was unprofessional and out of line."

(2) Apologize.

An apology is when you verbally ask the person you have offended to forgive you for your offensive comments or inappropriate behaviors. Your apology becomes believable when your actions support your request; in other words, when you stop making offensive comments and behaving inappropriately. If you ask and seek forgiveness, but you continue making offensive comments and behaving inappropriately, your initial request will be forfeited and perceived as fake and insincere.

When referencing the previous story, Jerry could apologize to Glen by saying, "Glen, I am sorry for using derogatory, demeaning and disrespectful language towards the gay couple the other day. Would you please forgive me for my offensive comments and inappropriate behaviors towards you and the gay couple? I acknowledge what I did; please accept my apology."

The longer it takes for you to apologize when you have offended someone, the more you will be perceived as an uncaring person. People may immediately refer to you as a racist, a sexist, a homophobic person or someone who is intolerant of differences, especially when the offense is diversity-related. Time does matter when you have offended someone, and an apology delivered and offered in a timely manner is critical to healing and rebuilding broken relationships. The longer a person has to wait for an apology, the larger the divide grows between you and the person you offended.

Rebuilding diversity trust does require that you interact with the person you have offended. You need their participation to rectify the situation. Consider asking the following questions as you seek to reconcile with the person you have offended:

- "What changes would you like to *see* in my *behaviors*?"

- "What words or phrases would you like for me to *eliminate* from my vocabulary?"

- "What *attitudinal* changes do I need to make to rebuild trust with you?"

- "What do I need to *do* for you to trust me again?"

Trust me on this piece of diversity-related advice. You will always be more effective in resolving diversity conflict and tension when you involve the person you have offended in the process.

(3) Behave Your Way Out of the Mess You Behaved Your Way Into.

I was first introduced to this concept when I attended a daylong leadership summit on June 15, 2005, in Saint Paul, Minnesota. One of my favorite scholars and author of the best-selling books, *The 7 Habits of Highly Effective People* and *The 8th Habit*, Dr. Stephen R. Covey made a profound statement that day, which changed how I viewed the process of forgiveness. Dr. Covey stated, "You cannot talk your way out of a mess you behaved your way into."

Most Americans are told early in life that actions speak louder than words. In other words, people will not believe your words if your actions do not match your words. Do you practice what you preach? Matching your words with your behaviors is known as congruency in the field of interpersonal communication. ***Congruency is when your words and actions are in alignment with one another.*** When you hurt someone due to offensive comments and inappropriate behaviors, it is important to verbally apologize, but your sincerity will be determined by your actions. In other words, did you stop making the offensive comments and behaving inappropriately?

As Dr. Covey instructed, your words will not rectify the situation alone; you have to behave your way out of the mess you behaved yourself into. If comments created the diversity conflict and tension, you will need to use appropriate language to correct the situation. If certain behaviors led to the diversity conflict and tension, you will need to behave in a more respectful manner to rebuild diversity trust. If you apologized, but you have not changed your ways, your behaviors will be seen as incongruent to the offended person. When your actions and behaviors are congruent, you will have begun the process of rebuilding the diversity trust that was initially lost.

(4) Be Consistent and Respectful with Your Words and Behaviors.

When you commit to correcting your diversity-related offenses, you are making a promise to eliminate making offensive comments and behaving inappropriately. If your words and behaviors do not change, you will be unable to rebuild diversity trust. To rebuild diversity trust, you must be fully dedicated and devoted to routinely doing the right thing. Will you be under the microscope? Absolutely! You must remember—you offended someone or a group of people with offensive words and behaviors, so they are checking to see how authentic and sincere you are as a person. They want to know if you are really sorry and if you have really learned your lesson. This is your opportunity to reinvent yourself, both personally and professionally. Will you or won't you rise to the occasion?

Do you have to be perfect now? Remember, no one is perfect. We all make diversity-related mistakes intentionally and unintentionally. However, when you make a diversity-related mistake, immediately and sincerely acknowledge and admit to your offensive words or inappropriate behaviors. While you are on your diversity journey or quest, remember that you are not perfect. A diversity journey and quest both imply that you will be *learning*, *unlearning* and *relearning* information.

(5) Befriend Time and Patience (This is Critical to Rebuilding Diversity Trust).

Some people believe that time heals all wounds. I do not believe time heals *all* wounds. I believe diversity wounds can be healed when the person who was hurt and violated is deliberate, intentional and proactive about practicing the behavioral skill of diversity forgiveness. The offender may ask, "How long will it take for the offended person to forgive me for my offensive comment or inappropriate behavior?" Diversity forgiveness depends on three variables: (1) how quickly the person who committed the offense acknowledges, admits and apologizes for her or his offensive comment or inappropriate behavior, (2) how quickly the person who committed the offense stops making offensive comments and behaving inappropriately and (3) how willing the person who was offended is to practice diversity forgiveness and move forward.

How Long Does Diversity Forgiveness Take?

"I'm sorry! I'm *really* sorry! I didn't mean anything by it. It was only a joke," lamented a young man after he personally offended and professionally punctured several workplace relationships due to an inappropriate and offensive e-mail. This is a classic case of someone defending their intentions without regarding how the impact of their behaviors will affect others. Perhaps the joke was designed to prompt a little humor in the workplace after a stressful team meeting. However, the aftermath was a group of offended colleagues and employees trying to make sense out of what they perceive as nonsense. How long will it take for the offender's colleagues to forgive him of his inappropriateness and offensiveness?

Consider the perspective of one of my favorite authors and books, Don Miguel Ruiz's, *The Four Agreements*, when he addresses the issue of forgiveness, writing:

> *"How many times do we pay for one mistake? The answer is thousands of times. The human is the only animal on earth that pays a thousand times for the same mistake. The rest of the animals pay once for every mistake they make. But not us. We have a powerful memory. We make a mistake, we judge ourselves, we find ourselves guilty, and we punish ourselves. If justice exists, then that was enough; we don't need to do it again.*
>
> *But every time we remember, we judge ourselves again, we are guilty again, and we punish ourselves again, and again, and again. If we have a wife or husband, he or she also reminds us of the mistake, so we can judge ourselves again, punish ourselves again, and find ourselves guilty again. Is this fair? Every time we remember the mistake, we blame them again and send them all the emotional poison we feel from the injustice, and then we make them pay again for the same mistake. Is that justice? True **justice** is paying only once for each mistake. True **injustice** is paying more than once for each mistake."*

Diversity forgiveness is a combination of forgiving those who have offended us as well as the offenders forgiving themselves of the offenses that they have committed against an individual or a group of people. I feel fortunate to have met and witnessed one of the greatest illustrations of diversity forgiveness a few years ago in Cleveland, Ohio. I was invited to present at a huge professional association event. One of the featured speakers was the daughter of James Byrd, Jr. (the black man dragged to death in Jasper, Texas, by a group of racist white men). She showed video clips of her father just being a fun loving and jokester kind of father. The clips showed Mr. Byrd singing as he played the piano for his family members and friends. There were about 2,000 conference attendees. The phrase, 'You could hear a pin drop' in the room was very appropriate and fitting during her time on stage. As I scanned the audience, there was a myriad of emotions being expressed: some people were crying, some people were shaking their heads with motions of disgust and disbelief and others were simply frozen with no expression at all. She played video clips of the men who were responsible for the heinous hate crime. After the clip of the three men in the courtroom she said to the audience, "I wanted to hate them for killing my father. I was angry. I'm quite sure you would be angry. But I forgave them. I forgave all of them. I've even corresponded with them through letters. Yes, everyone, I forgave them."

It was at this moment that I began to cultivate the philosophy and practical skill of diversity forgiveness. It was after this event that I began to incorporate and teach the philosophy and practice of diversity forgiveness into my *Be Diversity Competent* workshops. Byrd's daughter has gone on to work with political leaders to change legislation regarding hate crimes in America. She knew she could not live a fully engaged life if she spent her life full of diversity grudges, hate and resentment.

> "True justice is paying only once for each mistake. True injustice is paying more than once for each mistake."
> **Don Miguel Ruiz**

If you have offended someone, please understand that there is no exact science to when you will be forgiven. You cannot rush the diversity trust process because diversity trust is built when positive encounters and experiences occur over a period of time. Diversity trust is built one interaction at a time. The hard truth about rebuilding diversity trust is that it is easier to lose diversity trust than it is to rebuild diversity trust. Remember–you must behave your way out the diversity mess that you behaved yourself into. I know this may seem overwhelming, but if you persist in doing the right thing, you can rectify most personal and professional problems you may have caused. I wish you good success on your journey of rebuilding diversity trust!

Communicative Skills

There were many childhood songs and chants my friends and I shouted as we played outdoors on the west side of Chicago. There is one chant, in particular, that I used as a defense mechanism whenever my friends' 'Yo momma' jokes were more cutting and funnier than mine. I would sing and chant, "Sticks and stones may break my bones, but words will never hurt me." Of course this childhood song and chant is not true because words *do* hurt, and they can be very cutting and painful whether they are used intentionally or unintentionally. The philosophy and practice of diversity competence teaches us that in order to communicate and interact appropriately and effectively with diverse people, one must use appropriate, inclusive and respectful diversity language.

What does an individual's diversity vocabulary say about them? The language an individual employs during an interpersonal encounter communicates volumes regarding their level of diversity awareness and cultural sensitivity. When you use inclusive language, it affirms the diversity and humanity of other human beings. The individuals you communicate and interact with may be very sensitive about the adjectives you use to describe them. The diversity language you use can either be a *deal maker* or a *deal breaker.* How would you personally and professionally rate your diversity vocabulary? Have you recently updated and upgraded your diversity vocabulary? Do the words you use while communicating and interacting with diverse people degrade, demean, exclude, insult or offend people on the basis of disability, race, ethnicity, age, gender, religious practice or sexual orientation?

When a diversity competent individual uses inclusive diversity language, she or he is using diversity-friendly and welcoming language that is non-discriminatory. The language that you use will determine if diversity bridges are built or destroyed in your personal and professional relationships. Your diversity vocabulary may include words, phrases and expressions that are inclusive or exclusive, respectful or disrespectful, uplifting or demeaning. It does not matter if you did not mean to say what you said because people cannot see your intentions when you use offensive language, but they do feel the sting and impact of your offensive words and language. It is imperative that you consistently update and upgrade your diversity vocabulary as times change and as our world becomes more and more diverse. There is no need to fret because updating and upgrading your diversity vocabulary is an ongoing and life-long process. Again, I wish you good success on your diversity quest as you enhance and improve your diversity vocabulary!

Communicative Skill #1
Be Aware of and Self-Monitor Your 7%

Can a listener determine your level of diversity competence by your choice of words during a conversation with diverse people? You better believe it! The selection of words you choose to employ during a diversity encounter will communicate your level of knowledge regarding inclusive and exclusive diversity language. This is what Dr. Albert Mehrabian of UCLA meant when his research stated, "Seven percent of a message is received and understood by choice of words." The 7% that you employ in life, school and work will contribute to the diversity climate you create while communicating and interacting with diverse people. The words you use can lead to chaos and conflict or effective communication and cooperation. Using appropriate words, language and expressions are critical to creating diversity-friendly, inclusive and welcoming schools and organizations.

As I stated earlier, updating and upgrading your diversity vocabulary is a life-long diversity quest. What is the best way to update and upgrade your diversity vocabulary? I often suggest that individuals read credible and reputable newspapers and magazines that are diversity-friendly, inclusive and welcoming. As you read the stories in these publications, you will most likely see the usage of appropriate and current inclusive language. I suggest watching and listening to various news channels and reporters to learn which kind of diversity language to use when addressing diverse individuals and groups.

Please do not allow these communication mediums to be your *only* form of education and information as you learn to communicate more effectively with diverse people. The most effective way of communicating appropriately with diverse individuals is to simply ***ask*** the person you are communicating with how she or he would like to be addressed. Sometimes there are members of the same cultural community and ethnic group who disagree on what they would like to be called. When in doubt ask, ask and ask. You are only then guaranteed to communicate appropriately and effectively, at least with that particular person.

Consider the following words as you replace outdated language with updated and upgraded language (this is only a partial list to illustrate a point).

Exclusive and Outdated Diversity Language	Inclusive and Updated Diversity Language
Minorities	People of Color or Americans of Color
Orientals	Asian or Asian American
Retarded or Imbeciles	Persons with Mental or Cognitive Challenges
Homosexual	Members of the GLBT community
Sexual Preference	Sexual Orientation
Negro or Colored	Black or African-American
Handicapped or Disabled	Persons with Disabilities or Persons with Physical Disabilities
Hard of Hearing or The Deaf	People who are Hearing Impaired
The Blind or Blind People	People who are Blind or Visually Impaired
AIDS Victim	A Person who is HIV Positive or Persons Living with HIV/AIDS
Cripple or Wheelchair Bound	A Person who Uses a Wheelchair or A Person with a Mobility Impairment

As you can see, some terms that were considered appropriate to use some decades ago are no longer considered to be appropriate when addressing and discussing diversity-related topics and issues. You will need to continue to update your diversity vocabulary as our schools, organizations and society becomes more and more diverse.

Communicative Skill #2
Reduce Diversity Anxiety and Uncertainty

The feelings and thoughts you hold of other cultures and diverse people will determine your level of communication and interaction with them. If your feelings and thoughts are favorable towards their unique diversity, you will find yourself willing to freely engage in dialogue and discussion. If your feelings and thoughts are unfavorable towards their unique diversity, you will find yourself avoiding contact, dialogue and discussion. The latter of these perspectives is why I was compelled and motivated to write *Be Diversity Competent*. My personal and professional goal is to help individuals and organizations overcome or significantly reduce their Diversity BAPS (Biases, Assumptions, Prejudices and Stereotypes) when communicating and interacting with diverse people.

Do you *feel* or have you ever *thought* to yourself:

• Asians are quiet and shy, and they only stick to their own kind.

• Black women are angry and feisty.

• White police officers have it out for people of color.

• Gays and lesbians are flirtatious and promiscuous.

• Christians are closed-minded.

• Elderly people are stubborn and hard to get along with.

• Jewish people are cheapskates and penny pinchers.

• Native Americans are alcoholics.

• Teenagers are disrespectful and irresponsible.

• Italians and Irish people all have some sort of mob connection.

• Students of color are not as intelligent as white students.

• Persons with disabilities are not as effective and efficient as "able" bodied people.

Our Diversity BAPS get in the way of relationship building every single day. If you do not have any personal experience or knowledge of a specific culture or diverse group, you tend to rely on what others (such as our parents, guardians, family members, friends and of course the media) have taught you regarding the specific cultural or diverse group. Diversity anxiety and uncertainty is high in the beginning because we do not know what to *expect* from the people who are different from us, nor do we know how to *behave* in the presence of those who are different from us.

Not knowing what to expect and not knowing how to behave are two root causes of diversity anxiety and uncertainty. Human beings communicate and interact better with diverse people when they feel at ease and safe during the communication process. This is why Diversity BAPS prevent relationship building with diverse people from occurring because the feelings and thoughts we hold of diverse people are so negative that we feel uncomfortable and nervous during the communication process. Those who possess a high level of diversity anxiety and uncertainty typically anticipate something *bad* is going to happen when communicating and interacting with diverse people they are not familiar with.

Do you find yourself feeling awkward, uneasy or uncomfortable when communicating and interacting with unfamiliar diversity? If so, you are not alone! It is not abnormal to feel socially awkward and interpersonally incompetent when communicating and interacting with diverse people you have very little experience with. Even though you feel awkward, it is important for you to know that it is *impossible* to build healthy and positive diversity relationships with diverse people if you have high levels of anxiety and uncertainty regarding their unique diversity.

For example, if you recall the story I shared in part one of the book titled, "Don't Judge A Book by Its Cover: The Jon Lauer Story," initially I did not allow myself to get to know Jon Lauer because of the high level of anxiety and uncertainty

I held of his unique diversity; remember, Jon Lauer is white. I allowed Uncle Ricky's negative perceptions of white people to taint and distort my perceptions of how I viewed Jon. My Diversity BAPS hindered my relationship with Jon early on. I was not able to communicate and interact competently with Jon until I reduced my diversity anxiety and uncertainty of his unique diversity.

So what is diversity anxiety and uncertainty? Simply, *diversity anxiety and uncertainty are negative feelings and thoughts that a person experiences as a result of not being familiar with another person's unique diversity.* A high level of diversity anxiety and uncertainty prevents relationship building, especially when diversity is a variable. Diverse relationship building does not take place until individuals and organizations practice the diversity skill of reducing diversity anxiety and uncertainty.

So what does it mean to reduce diversity anxiety and uncertainty? *Reducing diversity anxiety and uncertainty is the deliberate process of getting to know diverse people by practicing the DALO Approach*, which is mentioned earlier in the book (part two). Once again, the DALO Approach is an interpersonal communication tool that is designed to help individuals learn more about the diverse people they are communicating and interacting with on a regular basis. The DALO Approach (Dialogue, Ask Questions, Listen and Observe) is a great tool to employ when the communication goal is to reduce diversity anxiety and uncertainty.

The DALO Approach allows individuals to look for common ground and similarities during the communication process. It is easier to communicate and get along with diverse people when there are similarities that exist between you and them. The DALO Approach does not have to follow any particular order or format; the goal of this interpersonal communication tool is to help people get to know one another better. You will find as you reduce diversity anxiety and uncertainty that you will begin to ask more personal questions. This is due to the fact that you have significantly reduced the fear and discomfort in the relationship, which are key barriers to building healthy and positive diverse relationships.

All diverse relationships begin with a friendly smile and a positive greeting. I believe the only way to get to know a person is to really *get to know a person*. Yes, you can overcome your diversity awkwardness and uneasiness; however, building any kind of new relationship does require time, energy, effort and commitment. Any quality-based interpersonal relationship is developed over a period of time. There is no such thing as an overnight relationship. Yes, it is possible to have an immediate connection with someone, but that relationship must still be cultivated on a regular basis. Each person must be *willing* to get to know one another.

A Stranger in the House—The Naim and Neelah Story

My eldest brother Andraé lives in Jacksonville, Florida. I had a brand new niece and nephew, whom I had only seen once when they came to Chicago. I decided one summer to spend ten days in Florida to get acquainted with my nephew, Naim, and my niece, Neelah. Once there, I greeted the family excitedly and they returned my greeting with equal excitement. All except my nephew Naim, who watched me from a distance, never drawing close. Desiring to know him better, I was taken aback by his apprehension, hesitation and resistance.

Days went by, but still my nephew Naim would not come close to me. In fact, the more I tried to gain his affection and attention, the more he backed away. Instead, he observantly watched me from a distance. My niece came and sat with me, but still Naim did not. Almost a week passed with him watching as I interacted with his mother, father and other siblings. I realized he was trying to reduce his diversity anxiety and uncertainty. He was observing me until he felt more comfortable, and eventually, he came to me. I was playing a video game with his sister, and I felt a pat on my leg. Finally, he climbed onto my lap. From that day on, we communicated and interacted without any problems.

Naim had been feeling me out until he had reduced his anxiety and uncertainty enough to approach me. In Naim's eyes, I was considered new diversity in his home, so he was fearful and uncertain until he reduced his diversity fear and uncertainty of me. As adults, what can we learn from little Naim's story?

Communicative Skill #3
Eliminate Language Barriers

You may be wondering how a person can communicate effectively with diverse people when language barriers exist. This is one of the most popular asked questions during my *Be Diversity Competent* workshops. I agree you cannot communicate appropriately and effectively with people when you do not understand them and they do not understand you. As a result of the above question, I have developed a five-step process that will increase your success rate when you communicate and interact with non-native speakers of English.

This five-step process will not eliminate all your communication challenges, but it will increase your probability of connecting with others while significantly reducing any language barriers that exist between you and the non-native speakers of English. Communication challenges do not have to leave you feeling agitated, frustrated and irritated. You can overcome these dreadful feelings as you become a more competent communicator.

The Five Step Process of Eliminating Language Barriers

Step 1: Speak with Clarity

Do you articulate, enunciate and pronunciate clearly when communicating with diverse people? Your clarity level during diversity encounters and interactions can determine if your words are *clearly* understood or *grossly* misunderstood. If your words are not clear, you will be unsuccessful at communicating effectively with non-native speakers of English. Remember, successful communicators accomplish their communication goals while interacting with diverse people and specifically non-native speakers of English.

The faster an individual speaks, the more clarity becomes a necessity to ensure effective communication. Fast talking individuals must be conscious of their articulation, enunciation and pronunciation because they run the risk of their words running together and saliva building up in their mouth while talking which interferes with clear communication. When speakers run their words together, they speak gibberish, which means their words do not make sense to others due to poor articulation, enunciation and pronunciation. Here are a few examples of gibberish being spoken as a result of poor articulation, enunciation and pronunciation and also a few examples of clear articulation, enunciation and pronunciation using Standard American English:

Gibberish	Standard American English
Didjaeetyet?	Did you eat yet?
Whatdjasay?	What did you say?
Whadayado?	What do you do
Offen	Often
Illinoi	Illinois
Evning	Evening
Gov-a-ment	Gov-ern-ment
Hi-stry	Hi-story
Wader	Waiter
Dese	These
Acrost	Across
Athalete	Athlete
Wanna	Want to
Comp-ny	Comp-a-ny
Beder	Better
Idear	Idea
Wanna	Want to
Soun	Sound
Wep	Wept
Wh-fect	Effect
Go-in	Going

Perhaps, I should also mention that speaking with gum, candy and food in your mouth definitely interferes with great articulation, enunciation and pronunciation. It is easier to understand a person when you can *hear* and *understand* the person.

Remember, your goal is to make your messages clear and easily understood by the person you are communicating with. The easier it is for the receiver to understand you, the higher your chances of having a great conversation. Of course clear communication is a win-win for both the speaker and the receiver.

Step 2: Respectfully Speak Slower

Do you talk too fast or do others listen too slowly? Talking too fast or listening too slowly is not the real problem. The real problem occurs when the speaker and the listener are not on the same rhythmic pattern during the communication process. One way to ensure that the speaker and the listener end up on the same rhythmic pattern is for the speaker to respectfully speak slower when she or he first enters into a dialogue. Why should you respectfully speak slower initially? Besides simply being cordial toward other human beings, speaking slower allows the listener to become familiar with your speaking rate and pattern. When the listener becomes familiar with your speaking rate and pattern, it becomes easier for them to follow the conversation, which eventually increases comprehension and understanding. Speaking a little slower allows the listener to adjust to differences in your accent, dialect, speech and choices of words during the interaction. Remember–clear communication leads to a clear understanding.

According to Adler, Proctor and Towne, "The average person speaks between 100 to 150 words per minute." It is important to understand that your speaking rate may be too fast for listeners to rapidly process and understand. For non-native speakers of English, she or he must first make sense of your message in their native language as well as in English, which implies some non-native speakers of English may take a little longer to process and make sense of your message.

As a communications professor, I have worked with more than 3,000 public speaking students over the last ten years, and many former students who were non-native speakers of English have shared with me that they have multiple translations going on inside their heads. I have observed how difficult, embarrassing and frustrating this process has been for many of them. How can this piece of information benefit you as a communicator? Please keep in

> "Nothing can be loved or hated unless it is first known."
> **Leonardo Da Vinci**

mind the virtue of patience when communicating and interacting with diverse people whose primary language is *not* English. Patience is critical to ensuring effective communication when language barriers exist. You may have to repeat yourself several times in a respectful manner and slower speaking rate to ensure that the person understands your statement or request.

Speaking slower does not imply speaking slower in a degrading, demeaning and disrespectful manner. Once during one of my *Be Diversity Competent* workshops, a woman revealed one of her Diversity BAPS (Biases, Assumptions, Prejudices and Stereotypes). She said [of non-native speakers of English], "I tend to think they are uneducated, poor and slow [cognitively challenged or mentally delayed]." I responded by saying, "Proficiency of any language requires time. Mastery of any language requires time. It is a great misnomer to believe non-native speakers of English are uneducated as a result of not mastering the English language as quickly as you think that they should."

In reality, many immigrants and refugees who come to the United States typically speak multiple languages other than English. Therefore, the acquisition of two or more languages does convey a regard for education and academic achievement. Best selling author and diversity expert, Sondra Thiederman, Ph.D., dispels stereotypes of non-native speakers of English, termed "intellectual inferiority" in her book, *Getting Culture Smart*. She writes, "Remember: The presence of a foreign accent says little about the speaker's ability to understand, read, write and speak perfect English vocabulary and grammar. An accent is only the way the words are pronounced."

To reiterate, non-native English speakers come to the U.S. with an array of knowledge regarding language. In going with this notion, there is a running joke in the world of diversity training. The joke brings up the issue as to who, Americans or immigrants, are acquiring and learning more languages and becoming more cultured as a collective group of people?

Consider the moral of the story as you read the following joke:

What do you call a person who speaks three or more languages?	*Multi-lingual*
What do you call a person who speaks two languages?	*Bi-lingual*
What do you call a person who speaks *only* one language?	*An American*

When I first heard the joke, I thought that it was not your typical joke. I see this "joke" as more of a rhetorical question to provoke introspective thinking as well as to challenge stereotypes some Americans hold of immigrants and non-native speakers of English. I believe the author or authors of this "joke" were attempting to dispel the stereotypes of immigrants being uneducated and intellectually incompetent and inferior.

The dispelling of that narrow opinion brings up another important point. Learning a language takes time. Consider practicing cognitive complexity and empathy when communicating and interacting with non-native speakers of English. What would your experience be like if you were learning a new language in a new country? Would you communicate with confidence and ease while under pressure? How much patience would you need from others as you practice and learn a new language? How many mistakes would you make in the communication process?

The Loud Factor: Screaming and Yelling

How degrading and embarrassing for a non-native speaker of English when another speaker screams and yells verbs, nouns and adjectives at them because the conversation is not going as expected? How many times have you witnessed this kind of ineffective interpersonal communication taking place? I have witnessed the Loud Factor taking place far too many times when language barriers exist. *The Loud Factor is when a speaker, raises her or his voice volume as a result of agitation, frustration and irritation while communicating and interacting with non-native speakers of English.* When speakers use the Loud Factor as a form of communication, it does not ensure effective communication. Instead, it inadvertently creates a larger divide between both parties. Screaming and yelling at non-native speakers of English will only embarrass, insult, intimidate and offend them. Additionally, the Loud Factor does not guarantee message comprehension. Screaming and yelling actually confuses and disorientates the listener, which of course leads to failed comprehension and communication. Great communicators use an appropriate and respectful voice volume that is suitable for the person she or he is communicating and interacting with.

Language barriers and challenges are difficult at times, but that does not mean communication is doomed. Your DA (diversity attitude) will determine how you communicate with non-native speakers of English. What is your DA when communicating with diverse people who have not mastered the English language? Do you have a DA of apathy, sympathy or empathy? How will each kind of DA affect relationship building and your interactions with non-native speakers of English? Write your answers down as you strive to become more diversity competent.

Step 3: Avoid the Use of Clichés, Jargon and Slang

A few years ago, I was teaching on the topic of appropriate language use in my Introduction to Public Speaking class, and an African student shared the following story with the class:

American Interviewer:	"How long have you been in the U.S.?"
African Student:	"About eight weeks."
American Interviewer:	"I see. So you're fresh off the boat?"
African Student:	"No, I flew."

This story reveals a communication breakdown as a result of a language barrier. This story is a classic case of how using clichés, jargon and slang while communicating with non-native speakers of English can lead to unsuccessful communication. Effective communicators accomplish their communication goals by using appropriate and inclusive language. Clichés, jargon and slang are only appropriate and effective when the individuals you are communicating and interacting with understand your colloquialisms.

Clichés, jargon and slang are everywhere within the American culture and American language system. These communication short hands allow us to connect a little easier and quicker with the people in our personal and professional lives. When the listener does not understand them, these short hands make the communication process complicated and difficult.

Step 4: Use Non-verbal Communication Gestures

Why should you use gestures when communicating important messages to non-native speakers of English? The answer is simply to ensure effective communication. ***Gesturing is a form a communication that individuals use when talking with their arms, fingers and hands.*** Using gestures when language barriers exist can significantly reduce communication breakdowns and misunderstandings. Non-verbal gestures will help you clearly illustrate and reinforce your verbal messages.

For example:

- When you say to someone, "Please sign your name on the dotted line." Effective gesturing is pointing to the dotted line while verbally saying it.

- When providing directions you say, "The human resource office is on this floor after you make the first right turn upon leaving this office." Effective gesturing is pointing forward to communicate directions as well as gesturing with your fingers or hand exactly where the person should make the correct right turn.

Employing non-verbal gestures while communicating with non-native speakers of English reinforces your key messages, allowing them to be quickly grasped and fully understood.

Step 5: Ask Questions for Clarity

It was my final semester of graduate school at the University of Wisconsin-Superior, and I was eager to take a journalism class. As my journalism professor, Mike Simonson, lectured on the first day of class, I was captivated by a quote that I will never forget. Professor Simonson lectured, "When covering any kind of newsworthy story, make sure you address and answer the following questions: who, what, when, where, why and how—this is called the five Ws and the one H."

I experienced an *Ah-Ha* moment when he stated, "All I ever learned in life I was taught by who, what, when, where, why and how—the five Ws and the one H." I thought to myself, *yes, that's how a person grows and develops in life...by asking questions.* The desire and will to ask questions while exploring one's diversity journey is paramount to becoming diversity competent. Asking questions implies that you have a spirit of inquisition and exploration.

When communicating and interacting with non-native speakers of English, keep in mind you will have to ask questions to ensure clarity of communication with the person you are interacting with. The goal of effective communication is to be both *heard* and *understood*. It is okay to respectfully ask the person to repeat their messages or requests. Remember, you cannot help someone if you do not understand her or his problems, concerns or issues. It is normal in the communication process to ask a person, "Would you be willing to speak a little louder so I can help you with your request? Thank you very much!"

The Embarrassment Factor

How many times should you ask a non-native speaker of English to repeat themselves? This has been debated from various angles and perspectives. If your goal is to truly assist and help the person, then I think your goals as a communicator and working professional will determine how many times you ask the person to repeat themselves. Please keep in mind that the more you ask them to repeat themselves, the more embarrassment the person will probably experience. When people feel embarrassed during the communication process, they tend to agree with you even when they do not understand you. It is not a sign of disrespect towards you, but rather, the person who is embarrassed is attempting to reduce their level of embarrassment. Sometimes you may even notice the person smiling as they verbally agree with you, even if they really do not understand you. Once again, this is an attempt to reduce the embarrassment factor.

To help alleviate the above issue, Dr. Sandra Thiederman offers tips for assessing if your message has been understood by people whose primary language is not English. Dr. Thiederman writes:

- If the person has not asked any questions, there is a good chance that [she or he] did not understand enough of what you said to formulate a question.

- If the listener does not interrupt, [she or he] may not have understood what was being said.

- Perpetual nodding and smiling is probably intended just as a courtesy and may not indicate real understanding. Intermittent nodding is more of a positive sign.

- A blank expression may indicate lack of understanding although some cultures and some individuals tend to have what is known as a "low affect" or little facial expressions.

- Self-conscious laughter probably indicates that the person is trying to conceal his or her embarrassment at not understanding what you have said. If there is not an obvious reason for the person to be amused, regard laughter as a probable sign of confusion.

- Statements like, "I think I understand" often mean "I do not really understand, but I don't want to insult you by coming out and saying so." Be alert to tentative phrases like, "I think," "Pretty much" or "I believe I understand."

The five steps of eliminating language barriers were designed for you to improve and increase communication with diverse people and non-native speakers of English. The goal is to appropriately apply the five-steps and use those steps in any order you prefer.

As you grow and develop on your journey or quest of becoming more diversity competent, please consider Dr. Sondra Thiederman's tips and the five steps of eliminating language barriers. Good success to you and your organization as you develop effective communicative skills for diversity competence.

Mao-Lee's Story: Learn the Damn Language!

In December of 2002, after sixteen weeks of teaching, I had just wrapped up the last day of my Small Group Communication and Leadership course. As the students began to exit the classroom, they handed in their final 12-page paper.

Gathering my teaching supplies and heading back to my office, I heard my name called from behind me, and I turned to see one of my students, Mao-Lee. She held out an envelope, saying, "Professor Davis I would like you to have this card." Then she asked me to please open and read the card in front of her.

Opening the envelope and card, I read the words, "Thank you," written seven times.

I looked at Mao-Lee in shock, asking, "Why are you thanking me?"

Mao-Lee said, timidly, "I want to thank you for being extremely patient and understanding and for taking time with me before, during and after class to ensure my success in this course."

Mao-Lee was a 56-year-old woman from Vietnam, and English was not her native language, making her one of the many English-as-a-second-language learners enrolled at Century College. Mao-Lee had only been in the U.S. for three years and her English, though not great, was certainly not the worst I had encountered over the years. Mao-Lee knew English well enough to complete the course successfully.

Because I was aware of her language challenge, I respectfully spoke slower at times while teaching and providing homework assignments. I knew she might not relate easily to idioms regarding American culture, so I explained class assignments very carefully. Personally and professionally, I accepted this new diversity in my classroom because it reinforced one of my teaching philosophies—to be a student-centered professor as well as a content-centered professor.

I asked Mao-Lee again, "Why are you thanking me?"

She answered, "Some of my other professors are rude and insensitive. I know it's frustrating for them that I do not have full command of the English language, but Professor Davis, I'm doing my best. When I came to this country, I was 53; I had to learn a new language, a new diet, a new culture, a new geography, a new way of thinking and an entirely new culture. I'm thankful that you were patient and willing to understand my language challenges."

Immediately, I had put myself in Mao Lee's shoes (practicing cognitive complexity). Mentally, I began to question myself about how I would have reacted and fared in her situation. I began to think, *What if I had to uproot from the U.S. and move to Vietnam? What would that experience be like for me? How quickly could I learn the Vietnamese language?* Then, I thought about how difficult it must be to adjust to living in an entirely new environment. Just getting used to a new diet had to be hard. I imagined what it would be like if my favorite foods were not available, only foods that were very different than what I was used to eating. I was thinking, *No more soul food!* I had visions of my favorite dishes such as greens, cornbread, southern style macaroni and cheese and of course, sweet potato pie in my mind.

■   ■   ■

▪️ ◻️ ▪️ ◻️ Jermaine's Final Thoughts!

Hallelujah, hallelujah and hallelujah! Everyone, I have just completed *Be Diversity Competent*! This is a day and a moment of great cheer and jubilation. I thought hard, emoted deep and wrote from the inside out to equip the readers of this book with communication skills to help build cultural bridges despite our differences as unique individuals. I spent countless nights fighting writer's block, sitting in solitude, thinking and staring at either my desktop or laptop before I could pen a single word. Intermittently, I would rapidly write a sentence or a paragraph when a powerful thought registered in my heart or inside my head. These thoughts, ideas and principles were written in various locations such as my home, my car, airplanes, airports, various hotels, various Caribou Coffees, Starbuck's Coffees, Barnes and Noble and many independent coffee, tea and dessert shops.

Before I began writing *Be Diversity Competent*, I awakened abruptly one morning, and as I lay in bed staring at the ceiling, it was as if my heart, soul and emotions were asking me, "Jermaine, how will you make the world a better place today?" As I pondered, another question arose, "What contributions and gifts will you share with your generation before you die?" I immediately grabbed my Bic #2 mechanical pencil and began journaling on a white legal pad of paper. My first words were, "Change the world starting today, Jermaine, change the world starting today."

I must say that I was overcome with great emotion that particular morning. I began to think of how I must use the TAGS (Talents, Abilities, Gifts and Skills) that I have been blessed with to help make a positive change in the world. This is when I decided that writing *Be Diversity Competent* would be one of the many channels that I would use to help make the world a better place. For years, I had been using my TAGS of teaching and speaking to help individuals and organizations communicate more effectively with diverse people, but my biggest challenge would be capturing my ideas and feelings in written format.

Why write it? I want the messages inside *Be Diversity Competent* to reach people and places where I may never travel. I can only speak in so many cities, states and countries, but *Be Diversity Competent* could be in a different city, state or country, teaching folks while I am somewhere else in the world landing identical messages. This is what I call a true win-win situation. Most speeches contain a certain shelf life before they are forgotten or misplaced in the back of a listener's mind; however, a book with the same thoughts, ideas and principles can live a lifetime. Just think of some of your favorite authors, writers and poets who you have never met personally, but you have enjoyed and have gotten to know them through their written pieces. I want *Be Diversity Competent* to live forever. I wholeheartedly believe in the messages written inside of this book, and even when it is my time to leave Mother Earth, it is my heart's desire that these messages permeate future generations.

Furthermore, it has been my goal to challenge the readers to think about their attitude, behaviors and communication styles when communicating and interacting with diverse people. I would encourage each and every reader to make the necessary changes in their attitude, behaviors and communication styles if their diversity practices are unjust or unfair. I wrote *Be Diversity Competent* to provoke thought, evoke emotion and prompt healthy dialogues regarding diverse people as well as diversity-related concerns and issues. *Be Diversity Competent* was written to inspire leaders to be more deliberate about creating diversity-friendly, inclusive and welcoming schools and organizations. Importantly, students and employees are more engaged, effective and productive when both their cultural and individual diversity and humanity is affirmed.

Thank you for spending your time reading and studying *Be Diversity Competent*. Please teach the concepts, principles and practical tips written inside this book to your family members, friends and colleagues. Remember that diversity competence is a continuous journey and quest, so I encourage you to stay on your journey of learning to communicate appropriately and effectively with diverse people. It is my sincere hope and genuine expectation that you will be able to begin applying the techniques and strategies in this book immediately and that over time and with practice, you will be able to use all of them at once without any difficulty.

Congratulations for setting out on this important diversity journey and quest! I am confident that you will surmount old obstacles and traverse new ground by applying these skills. It is a life-long process, but one that I hope you will feel is worthwhile. Good success in all you do! Peacefully, Jermaine M. Davis.

■   ■   ■

■ ▢ ■ ▢ About the Author
Jermaine M. Davis

Jermaine M. Davis grew up in a single-parent home in Chicago's housing projects. After losing six family members to street violence, he began studying success principles to change the direction of his life. Now, Jermaine is the author of six books including: Get Up Off Your Butt & Do It NOW, Leading with Greatness, 207 STAND OUT Quotes to Help You Succeed in Life, School & Work, You Don't Have to SELL OUT to STAND OUT, Be Diversity Competent and Lessons from the Road.

Jermaine earned a BA and an MA in Speech Communication and completed a second MA in Education. He is a Professor of Communication Studies at Century College in Minnesota and has been presented with the prestigious College Instructor of the Year Award. Jermaine is also CEO, Founder and President of two companies: Seminars & Workshops, Inc. and Snack Attack Vending of Minnesota.

Before becoming a professor and CEO of two companies, Jermaine learned effective communication and leadership skills from organizations including IBM, Rolm Telecommunications, Frito Lay, Inc. and the Keebler Company. Although he left his corporate positions for a professorship, he continues to be active in the corporate world through his professional keynotes and workshops. Jermaine is one of the country's most requested inspirational teachers in the areas of diversity competence, leadership, team building and sustaining personal and professional motivation.

Jermaine is a Chicago native and presently resides in St. Paul, MN.

◼ ▢ ◼ ▢ A Special Invite
from the Author

If you would like to bring Jermaine M. Davis to your organization or school for a presentation or book signing, please contact our corporate office at:

Phone: (651) 487-7576

E-mail: jermaine@jermainedavis.com

Website: www.jermainedavis.com

To learn more about our discount program for resellers of *Be Diversity Competent!,* please contact our marketing and sales department at (651) 487-7576 or (773) 936-0222.

Here are the best ways Jermaine can help your organization succeed:

• Keynote and Endnote Presentations

• Executive and Managerial Coaching

• Public Speaking Coaching

• New Employee and Student Orientation Training

• Affinity and Employee Resource Group Training

• Faculty and Professional Staff Development Programs

• New Supervisor Coaching and Training

• Professional Association Conferences

• Parents' Day Programs

• Board of Director Training

• Teacher In-services

• Holiday Celebrations

• Award and Banquet Celebrations

• Student Leadership and Team Building Training

• Full-and Multi-Day Residencies

• Hall Directors and Residential Assistant Training

• Greek Life: Fraternity and Sorority Workshops

• Spiritual and Religious Conferences and Retreats

• Dr. Martin Luther King, Jr., Celebrations

• Diversity and Multicultural Celebrations and Events

Other Books By Jermaine M. Davis

Jermaine M. Davis Seminars & Workshops, Inc. is dedicated to providing personal and professional learning resources to help individuals and organizations accomplish their dreams, goals and aspirations. Consider adding the following books to your individual or organization's library.

▪ ▫ ▪ ▫ Other Books by Jermaine M. Davis

Get Up Off Your Butt & Do It NOW!

Written by Jermaine M. Davis

Leading with GREATNESS!

Written by Jermaine M. Davis

To Place an Order:

Website: www.jermainedavis.com

E-mail: jermaine@jermainedavis.com

Phone: (651) 487-7576

You Don't Have to SELL OUT to STAND OUT!

Written by Jermaine M. Davis
and Katie Ruberto

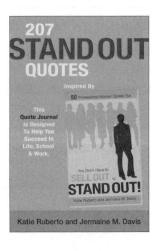

207 STAND OUT Quotes (The Ultimate Quote Journal)

Written by Jermaine M. Davis
and Katie Ruberto

Lessons from the Road

Written by Jermaine M. Davis and
Leading Speakers in Education

List the practical skills you've
added to your Communication
and Diversity Toolbox.

- _____

_____

- _____

_____

- _____

_____

- _____

_____

- _____

_____

- _____

_____

- _____

_____

- _____

_____

- _____

_____

Practice these skills daily to increase
your Diversity Competence.